ABOUT THE AUTHOR

MARIE WADDEN is the network producer for CBC Radio in
Newfoundland and Labrador. She has won prizes for her journalism in both Canada and the United States, and her research
for *Where the Pavement Ends* was made possible by one of the
country's most prestigious awards, the Atkinson Fellowship
in Public Policy. Her first book, *Nitassinan: The Innu Struggle
to Reclaim Their Homeland*, won the Edna Staebler Award for
Creative Non-fiction in 1991. Marie Wadden lives in St. John's,
Newfoundland, with her husband and their two children.

Canada's Aboriginal

Recovery Movement

and the Urgent Need

for Reconciliation

MARIE WADDEN

WHERE THE

PAVEMENT

ENDS

Douglas & McIntyre
D&M Publishers Inc.
VANCOUVER/TORONTO

Douglas & McIntyre
A division of D&M Publishers Inc.
2323 Quebec Street, Suite 201
Vancouver BC Canada V5T 4S7
www.dmpibooks.com

National Library of Canada Cataloguing in Publication Data
Wadden, Marie, 1955–
Where the pavement ends : Canada's aboriginal recovery movement
and the urgent need for reconciliation / Marie Wadden.
Includes index.

ISBN 978-1-55365-307-3 (cloth) · ISBN 978-1-55365-461-2 (paper)

1.Native peoples—Canada—Social conditions. 2.Native
peoples—Canada—Health and hygiene. 3.Native peoples—Substance
use—Canada. 4.Healing—Social aspects—Canada.
5.Native peoples—Canada—Government relations. I. Title.
E78.C2W125 2008   305.897′071   C2008-900406-X

Editing by Barbara Pulling
Jacket design by Peter Cocking and Naomi MacDougall
Text design by Naomi MacDougall
Jacket photograph © Getty Images/Baldur Bragason/Nordic Photos
Printed and bound in Canada by Friesens
Printed on acid-free paper that is forest friendly (100% post-consumer recycled paper)
and has been processed chlorine free.

We gratefully acknowledge the financial support of the Canada Council for the Arts,
the British Columbia Arts Council, the Province of British Columbia through the Book
Publishing Tax Credit and the Government of Canada through the Book Publishing
Industry Development Program (BPIDP) for our publishing activities.

This book is dedicated to

the memory of Rose Gregoire,

Apinam Pone and Gail Valaskakis,

individuals who dedicated

their lives to finding solutions.

Contents

Introduction

IN SEPTEMBER 1981, PETER PENASHUE AND EDWARD Nuna, two Innu teenagers from Sheshatshiu, Labrador, came to live in my three-storey, century-old house in St. John's. They were the only two students in their year to have reached grade eleven, and they'd come to St. John's to finish high school. In the ten months that followed, the three of us became friends, sharing confidences and weathering life's ups and downs. Peter and Edward trusted me to guide them through the daunting and unfamiliar territory of the city. In return, my life was enriched by their humour, their courage and the insights I gained into their ancient culture, shaped thousands of years ago by the northern Quebec and Labrador landscape. Innu history retains a memory of the Ice Age, and Peter and Edward's favourite story was about Tshakapesh, an Innu hunter who killed a mammoth to feed his people.

From Peter and Edward I learned too about the extent of alcoholism in Sheshatshiu. Edward was respectful of his parents, but their use of alcohol had prevented them from properly looking after their nine children, forcing him many times to go from house to house for food. Peter's family also struggled with alcoholism, but he exhibited greater self-confidence; his resilience came from his time in *nutshimit* (the country), where his family lived while his father and grandfather hunted. Sheshatshiu had not existed until the early 1960s; until then, most Innu still lived in tents and provided their own food by travelling over their land in canoes and toboggans. The move changed Peter's father, as it did so many others; in the new village, the able hunter became a drunk.

This was a riddle for me. How could a change in lifestyle produce such self-destructive behaviour from such fine people? I was invited to spend time with Peter and Edward's families, who treated me with great hospitality and kindness. From them I learned more about the dichotomy between life on the land and life in the village. Many households in Sheshatshiu were headed by alcoholics who were transformed on the land into hunting camp leaders, because they were such great providers of warmth and food. I became especially close to Peter's mother, Tshaukuesh (Elizabeth Penashue).

I moved to Montreal, where other interests preoccupied me. In 1987, while watching the news one evening, I was shocked to see a report from Labrador that showed Tshaukuesh and others being led away by police for hunting caribou illegally. Their actions were part of an organized protest by the Innu against provincial wildlife regulations that restricted the Innu to Sheshatshiu for most of the year—"as if we were in prison," Tshaukuesh later told me. Innu activism heated up even more when Canada announced its intention to build a NATO jet bomber training centre in Goose Bay. The people of Sheshatshiu had never signed a treaty or a land claims agreement with

Canada, and they feared that the frequent flights by jet bombers practising low-level flying and air-to-air combat training would do irreversible damage to caribou and other animals.

It was inspiring to see the Innu community come together with such passion to protect the environment. But their activism took great emotional energy, and by the late 1980s, the people of Sheshatshiu were bitter and exhausted by the political struggle. The younger generation had lost confidence in the traditional way of life but were left with little of spiritual or material value to replace it. A decade after the protests organized by their parents, young children in Sheshatshiu and Davis Inlet began routinely inhaling gasoline to get high. In many First Nations communities across the country, similar social problems had been evident for some time, often arising after people were forced off their traditional lands.

The catalyst for this book was an op-ed piece by John Gray that appeared in the *Globe and Mail* on March 8, 2005. Gray described the problems that the Innu people in the Labrador community, Davis Inlet, were having adjusting to their relocation to Natuashish, a community that had been built from scratch. There had been reports of more suicides and more solvent-abusing children, of financial corruption. It was Gray's last paragraph that goaded me into action. He wrote of his fear that these problems might have no solutions, that the lives of the Innu might never be better. "The disaster of Davis Inlet and Natuashish—and there are other Aboriginal communities across the country similarly afflicted—" he wrote, "is that nobody knows what to do."

In 2006, with the generous support of the Atkinson Charitable Foundation, I set out to look for people who *do* know what to do. My research, published as a series of stories in the *Toronto Star*, took me across the country, to Inuit communities in the Arctic and to First Nation and Metis communities from Labrador to British Columbia. Few of the communities I visited were marked on road maps or signposted on provincial highways. Often, I knew I'd come to the reserve because I had reached the end of the pavement.

At the outset of my journey, I was unaware of the incredible work Aboriginal people are doing in the area of addiction. A vibrant Aboriginal healing movement has sprung up, with recovery programs being created in many communities. Yet, despite their many successes, these programs are seriously underfunded and understaffed, placing their continued existence in jeopardy.

The situation could not be more urgent. After visiting Aboriginal communities, talking to numerous Aboriginal activists and reading dozens of books and countless reports, I have come to believe that the very survival of the first peoples of this country is at risk. Inuit women have raised the alarm about the high rates of violence in their communities. Experts on fetal alcohol spectrum disorder (FASD) warn of an impending social disaster if rates of alcohol abuse are not curtailed in Aboriginal communities. Sober people on reserves are begging for mental health and addiction training, and for income parity for the professionals who work in their communities. First Nations and Inuit leaders are calling for relief from a severe housing shortage and a national health budget that reflects the needs of the Aboriginal population. For Aboriginal people to take responsibility for their own lives, they need the political, moral support and financial support of the Canadian population. Figures released by Statistics Canada in January 2008 indicate just how critical the situation is. Over the past decade, the Aboriginal population in Canada has grown by 45 per cent; the average age of an Aboriginal person is twenty-seven, compared to an average of forty for non-Aboriginal Canadians. This is our country's most dynamic demographic, but our policies are not keeping pace with the challenges.

Much of the debate about solving "Aboriginal problems" revolves around public spending. Some non-Aboriginals are critical when they hear that $8 billion a year in federal money is spent on Canada's 1.5 million Aboriginal people. "Where's all our money going?" they ask. Aboriginal people have another way of looking at the issue of "our" money. They believe that it is being made off their land. Very little of that money comes back to them in effective ways, and what is provided is often first siphoned by the bureaucratic agencies that dispense it.

The pages of this book contain some answers. None of them are simple, since the problems are complex. Taken together, though, they outline some necessary steps on the path to finding solutions. Through Canada's Truth and Reconciliation Commission, which was launched in 2008, we have an opportunity to create a groundswell of support. The next five years will be crucial for raising public awareness about the damage done to Aboriginal society by the most egregious of Canadian government policies, the 1920 legislation that required First Nations parents to surrender their children to residential schools. We must make social healing in Aboriginal communities an immediate national priority. We must also demand public policy that guarantees First Nations, Inuit and Metis people the right to live as full and equal citizens. In these ways, we can offer true support to those committed to restoring health and happiness for the next generation.

Where the Pavement Ends could not have been written without the help of the many courageous Aboriginal people who told me their stories, exposing private sorrows in the hope that doing so will help others. The Penashue family has been particularly generous in allowing me to tell the story of their struggle for sobriety. Peter Penashue and Edward Nuna are sober leaders in their community today. I am blessed to know them.

Aboriginal people have accomplished much in their work to rebuild pride, culture and community. They need the active support of all Canadians to complete their journey. Our lives will be enriched by helping all people take their rightful place in this nation.

Healing the Spirit

ON A HOT, SUNNY AFTERNOON IN AUGUST 2006, A FIELD
of sorrows has been transformed into a field of celebration.
Acres of green grass bordered by softly waving deciduous
trees create a welcoming vista for the thousands of international guests attending one of the most unusual gatherings in
Canada.

Massive white tents have been placed here and there on
this field in St. Albert, a fertile farming area now a suburb of
Edmonton. People arrive by bus, then leisurely make their way
towards the tents, seeking shelter from the bright sun and the
comfort of a seat before the outdoor show begins. A stage has
been assembled in front of a two-storey brick building, previously known as the Edmonton Industrial School. The school
is an empty shell now, its windows boarded up. I imagine the
thousands of small children forced to climb the institution's
imposing concrete steps, heartbroken after leaving their parents and their home communities behind. It's no coincidence,

I think, that the stage has been placed so that performers will have their backs to the school, defying the oppression it represents. Surrounding me are Indigenous people from dozens of countries around the world. Many are in traditional dress, and the field that is now home to Poundmaker's Lodge and the Nechi Institute is awash in colours.

The most colourfully dressed delegates to this fifth Healing Our Spirit Worldwide gathering begin to assemble near two white teepees installed to one side of the stage. There's a hush among the spectators as a parade starts to form, soon snaking its way jauntily in front of the tents. Two beautiful First Nations fancy dancers twirl, their heads adorned with feathers, their long skirts swishing against their ankles, tiny bells jingling as they leap and turn. They are followed by a more sedate group of Hawaiians whose feet and legs are bare, their matching toga-style garments tied in a knot on their left shoulders. Fearsome-looking men carrying boomerangs have decorated their bare chests and faces with tattoos, and they keep their gazes forward as though heading into battle. There's a New Zealand Maori woman with a beard painted on her chin; she juts out her lower lip in a threatening fashion as her companions walk protectively beside her, wearing capes of woven grass.

Dallas Arcand, the Canadian Cree hoop-dancing champion, appears on stage, spinning dozens of hoops around his ankles, waist, wrists and neck. He performs some amazing contortions before bringing the hoops together in the shape of eagle wings as the last drumbeat signals his dance is over. As I wander among the crowd, I see more informal cultural exchange. An Australian Aborigine is grinning as she poses for a photo standing between two Canadian Mounties: one a tall First Nations man, the other a much shorter Inuit woman.

There is hilarity when the Mounties ask for their pictures to be taken beside two half-naked Maori warriors. Following the performances on stage are speeches by Canadian Aboriginal leaders such as Mary Simon of the Inuit Tapiriit Kanatami.

Large tables laden with food seem to have sprung from nowhere while our attention was focussed on the stage. Servers dish out copious quantities of wild rice, salmon, caribou meat, Saskatoon berries and a refreshing drink made from wild strawberries. The joyous mood is contagious. Some of the women serving food grab hold of one another to dance a jig. There is a lot of laughter and much intermingling. For this afternoon, anyway, the serious issues that have made this gathering necessary have dropped to the background, the 200-page conference agenda set aside until tomorrow. This party is the prelude to an international conference aimed at healing the world's Indigenous people from the ravages of addiction and social breakdown. It will be a full week.

The days that follow are packed with inspiring speeches and performances that emphasize the importance of taking responsibility for sobriety by drawing on the values of hard work, family unity and self-respect: values that colonial governments knocked out of Indigenous societies while trying to assimilate them, making them dependent and dysfunctional instead. Participants exchange information and propose solutions at hundreds of workshops about the social problems that are ripping Indigenous societies apart. There is a lively presentation from a group of Australian women who deliver addiction services to remote Aboriginal communities from a bus. Representatives from Canada's largest reserve, the Blood reserve in Alberta, explain how the community requires all of its public servants, from the garbage collector to the chief, to be drug and alcohol free. Alcohol and illegal drug addiction are not the only threat people have come to discuss. First Nations communities in Atlantic Canada, led by the Elsipogtog reserve in New Brunswick, had travelled to Ottawa two months earlier looking for help with a prescription drug abuse epidemic. "I've got forty residents looking for treatment now," Chief Susan Levi-Peters told me before I came here. "And they're just the people ready to acknowledge they have a problem." Gambling is a growing concern in many communities. There isn't room enough for all the people who want to attend a workshop called "Reducing the Risk of Child Molestation: Protecting the Next Generation." New Zealand Maori tell delegates how their peoples' well-being has improved since the creation of a Maori national health department. That's just one of the many possible solutions participants discuss. Each day opens and closes with euphoric cultural performances meant to build a spirit of hope and optimism. Aromatherapy, soft music and dreamcatchers are not on the agenda. The new age under discussion here is about building community life that is not dominated by addiction. A profound sense of urgency underlies everything.

During a coffee break, a diminutive Guatemalan woman in a fuchsia skirt, with an equally bright shawl draped across her shoulders, catches my eye. She is deep in conversation with a distinguished-looking man dressed in white from head to toe, except for his turquoise braided belt and red woven scarf. I learn they are part of a Mayan delegation here to explain how they are tackling youth suicide, a big problem for their people, too. A group of Australian Aborigines smile warmly at everyone who approaches them. One man wearing a cowboy hat greets me with a hearty handshake, his accent straight out of *Crocodile Dundee*. He introduces himself as Leo Abbott, a presenter at the conference. The tote bag he carries bears the words: "Strong Spirit, Strong Mind—Aboriginal ways to reduce harm from alcohol and other drugs." Next I strike up a conversation with a woman who gives me her card—Paretuaoroa Rata, health and social services manager for Te Runanga O Te Whanau, a Maori health agency. She's accompanying a youth delegation from her country, and she tells me how excited they are to see Canada for the first time. From the knowledgeable way she speaks, I suspect she's an influential player in New Zealand's health care field.

My conversation with Paretuaoroa is interrupted by the rustle of excitement on an outdoor landing that's part of the conference centre. The Hawaiian delegation has just carried a large canoe down to the North Saskatchewan River below us. "I don't know anything about Indigenous Hawaiians," I confess. Paretuaoroa tells me they are Polynesians, like the Maori, and related to other Indigenous people of the Pacific. The Hawaiians have brought this ceremonial canoe along to celebrate their tradition of seafaring.

As I chat, I'm also scanning the crowd for some sign of Maggie Hodgson, the Canadian woman who has brought all these people together. By the early 1970s, alcohol abuse in Aboriginal communities across Canada had reached crisis proportions, causing widespread chaos, hardship and death. Hodgson was among a committed group of First Nation individuals in Alberta, including a Saddle Lake Cree man named Eric Shirt, who started native addiction services because no one else was doing it. Shirt was instrumental in founding both Poundmaker's Lodge, the first treatment centre in Canada specifically for Aboriginal clients, and the Nechi Training, Research and Health Promotions Institute (*nechi* is the Cree

word for "friend"), which today trains drug and alcohol coun-
sellors from across North America and as far away as South
Africa and Sri Lanka. Maggie Hodgson served for fifteen years
as the institute's chief executive officer. In a powerful essay
entitled "From Anomie to Rebirth," published in 1992, Hodgson explains that the Aboriginal addiction recovery movement
is not a recent phenomenon. Hopi Indians in the nineteenth
century predicted that Indigenous North Americans would
come out of their darkness, or midnight, "when the Eagle
landed on the Moon." The astronauts who first walked on the
moon in 1969 famously used the words "the eagle has landed,"
and Aboriginal people such as Hodgson, aware of the proph-
ecy, took it as a hopeful sign.

"The Indian Alcohol Programs at that time were built on
the premise of re-introducing ritual, meaning of ritual, ceremony, healing, community and building a vision of sobriety,"
Hodgson writes. As Hodgson makes clear, they were also built
on hardship. "One woman in Alberta used to sell her bead-
ing to support herself while doing community workshops on
alcohol abuse. She often hitched a ride from community to
community. Another man, Chester Cunningham, mortgaged
his home to pay our alcohol education workers because Medical Services Branch had no policy by which they could fund
such a program. He had five children and a wife at home. Grit,
determination and courage. That was in 1971 and the commitment has grown to where we have communities moving across
Canada to a vision of sobriety."

Finally, I do spot Maggie in the crowd. Conference knap-
sack slung over one shoulder, her grey hair stylishly cut, she
is moving fast, trying to put out a small fire in the conference
procedures. She looks tired but exhilarated. "I was so excited

last night," she tells me, slightly out of breath. "I just couldn't sleep. I'd better pace myself this week."

Dr. Marjorie Hodgson's name is not a household name in Canada, but it should be. The sixty-two-year-old Nadleh Whuten Carrier woman from northern British Columbia is living proof of the power of one. The batteries that propel her, however, are wearing down. Maggie Hodgson has a heart condition, and she has already had three strokes.

Healing Our Spirit Worldwide was conceived by Hodgson sixteen years ago as a way to exchange ideas and bolster support among colonized people dealing with alcoholism. The gathering she has created is not just about addiction, though. It's about transforming oppression into exuberance. When we sit down to talk, I learn that this is the story of Hodgson's life.

Maggie Hodgson's birth family was poor, and her parents were alcoholic. When Maggie was a teenager in the 1960s, she was raped by a local businessman. The investigating RCMP officer told her mother not to expect more for her daughter. "You're an alcoholic and an Indian," he said, "and so is she. She's there to be used." Maggie was determined to prove him wrong. She'd learned all about defiance at the Roman Catholic boarding school she was sent away to attend.

"My response to boarding school was to become angry and resistant," Maggie says. "For thirty-two years I couldn't express my anger at Mom for sending me to a Catholic boarding school, because I had the Catholic philosophy of honouring your mother and father. So, if I couldn't express it to my mom, I turned it inward, and later at all the injustice I saw in society."

Maggie raged for a while. She had a nervous breakdown at the age of twenty-one and got well after some long-term therapy and participation in her people's traditional ceremonies.

Her experience became the catalyst for a worldwide Aboriginal sobriety and healing movement. Along the way, she came to believe that sobriety and social healing will spread faster among her people if they are able to move beyond their hatred over what happened to them. Once, in a workshop, she saw an Aboriginal man transformed by listening to the daughter of a white physician who had devoted his life to helping people in the North.

"The person had only ever had hatred for whites," Hodgson says, "and now he was learning about someone who cared very much for us."

As she worked through her own anger, Hodgson learned that injustice is never black and white. Maggie's mother had been forced by law to attend an Indian residential school. She in turn placed Maggie in a boarding school run by nuns. Hodgson hated the experience, but she has made peace with the religious people who ran the schools because she now believes many were themselves victims. Her insights allowed her to play a key role on the committee that recommended how the federal government should proceed with compensation for people sent to Indian residential schools.

Besides providing more than $1.9 billion in financial compensation for former students, the Indian Residential Schools Resolution Canada agreement provides funding for a national Truth and Reconciliation Commission that will hold hearings across the country starting in 2008. The agreement also provides for the establishment of memorials, commemorative events and programs to educate Canadians about the damage done to generations of Aboriginal people as a result of this heinous government policy.

In an essay entitled "Rebuilding Community after the Residential School Experience," Maggie Hodgson describes with compassion the plight of the Roman Catholic nuns who taught her. "Some really cared about the young people . . . ," she writes, "but had been trained in a system that taught harshness. They had been taught to sacrifice themselves, to deny their own loneliness and suppress their own humanity."

The first Healing Our Spirit Worldwide gathering was held in Edmonton in 1992. Hodgson helped create the event with Rod Jeffries, a Canadian Mohawk who has been at her side ever since. They'd both had experiences that made them realize non-Aboriginal solutions would not work for their people.

"We attended the international conference on addiction in Berlin in 1990," explains Jeffries. "They had included a track for Indigenous peoples. Once we got over there we found that it was not for us. The conference was very European, or Western, but it was also very academic, and we found that it didn't meet the needs of our people. So that's when we discussed having our own international conference, particularly around the area of alcohol and drug abuse."

So much enthusiasm developed among Australian Aborigines after the first Healing Our Spirit Worldwide conference that they offered to host another two years later. It's a lot of work for communities with a shortage of human and financial capacity, though. Since then the gathering has happened every four years, twice in Canada and once each in New Mexico, New Zealand and Australia. In 2010 it will take place in Hawaii.

It's impressive that Hodgson and her colleagues could set something as big as this in motion, but she has been doing things like that all her life, driven by a passion to heal her people. Her days are longer than most people's. She travels regularly between her home in Edmonton and Ottawa, where federal government policy-makers often seek her advice. These days she's a special advisor to Canada's Truth and Reconciliation Commission.

Hodgson's latest passion is building support for the National Day of Healing and Reconciliation on May 26 each year, a day she hopes will become as important to Canadians as her healing conference has become to Aboriginal people around the world. In fact, she's stepping down from active involvement with the International Indigenous Council that oversees Healing Our Spirit Worldwide to put her prodigious energy into reconciliation. The Truth and Reconciliation Commission will hold hearings for three years across the country but will also be doing a lot of work behind the scenes until 2012. Hodgson conceived the National Day of Healing and Reconciliation before the commission was founded, and she'd like it to continue after the commission's work is completed. Her aim? To help heal the rifts that have developed between Canada's non-Aboriginal and Aboriginal citizens.

Hodgson's idea for the national day was sparked by the kindness of a Chinese businessman who volunteered to help ease tensions during a serious confrontation between Aboriginal activists and the RCMP at Gustafsen Lake, British Columbia, in 1995. His actions made her realize the importance of widening the reconciliation and healing focus.

"We've said to non-Aboriginals for years, 'You need to listen to us more,' but now we need to listen to Canadians more," Hodgson says. "We need to listen to the Japanese Canadians, Ukrainian Canadians, Italian Canadians, German Canadians who have a history that is important that we know and understand. I think reconciliation is about reciprocity and respect."

The promotional booklet for the National Day of Reconciliation and Healing offers ideas on ways to bring together people who otherwise might not mix. "The campaign's intent is not to impose guilt on Canadians," the booklet explains.

"Healing is not an Aboriginal issue," Hodgson stresses. "It's a Canadian issue. If we Aboriginal people want others to know and support us, it's going to happen when we get interested in Canadians."

Hodgson wants the national day to bring reconciliation and healing to all groups. Right now, she feels Muslims are vulnerable. "I watched a Muslim woman roughed up at the airport recently," she tells me. "I felt strongly for what she was going through."

Hodgson has not received funding for the 2008 national day events and hopes the momentum created so far will not be lost.

The week I first met Hodgson, however, she was devoting herself to making sure things went well for the international delegates at Healing Our Spirit Worldwide. She knew many of them could barely afford to attend.

"I found a restaurant nearby that has a $4 breakfast," she interrupts our conversation to tell some fellow organizers. "Two strips of bacon, eggs and brown toast. Coffee is extra. I'll let people know about it."

Several times during the conference, I find myself seated beside Rod Jeffries's father, John Jeffries, who is a retired Anglican priest. I learn that the elder Jeffries was born on a Cree trapline and that he still presides over church services near his home in the Bay of Quinte, a Mohawk community at Tyendinaga, near Kingston, Ontario. He lives with his son Rod and his two grandsons. Reverend Jeffries tells me with great pride that, besides being an excellent public speaker, Rod is a talented fundraiser who secured nearly $1 million in contributions for one of these conferences. Later, I learn that Rod is past president of the National Association for Native American Children of Alcoholics and a consultant for Ancestral Visions, a company that provides wellness and development services.

"I had to deal with a lot of pain so that I could do the work I'm doing today," Rod tells me when we take a moment to chat. "Both my parents went to residential schools, and so there was a lot of hurt that they inadvertently passed on to us. For example, my father was in the school for ten years, so he grew up in an institution. He did not know what family was, and he passed that on. And he learned to hate the colour of his skin and the ways of his people. That was also passed on to us. I had to work through all those issues to be who I am today."

Other delegates speak out during the week on the damage caused by family breakdown. Nina Buckskin makes a startling declaration during a workshop explaining the federal government's $65 million strategy to prevent Aboriginal youth suicide, a program slated to run until 2010. Standing tall in the back of the room, she announces: "I think all the suicides in Aboriginal communities are caused by sexual abuse."

Buckskin is a retired teacher from the Blood reserve in Alberta. She is now an elected band councillor. "I worked for thirty-four years," she tells the group, "and many of the children would tell me stories about what was happening to them. You know, sometimes it's just unbelievable, the things that they told me. Imagine. We're expecting our children to come and learn, but when they have issues like that, how can they learn? A lot of suicides are happening on our reserve, and I believe sexual abuse is the number one cause. It's rampant. It's being done by grandpa, grandma, dad, brother, sister, cousin."

Later, Buckskin tells me she ran for council to help the children on her reserve. She recounts a story about a young man who confided in her how he noticed his uncle regularly take his sister away into the woods. One day he followed them, and he saw his uncle holding a pillow over his sister's mouth so she couldn't cry out for help as they disappeared into the bushes.

There are other surprising revelations for me. A young man originally from Kenya, Joe Gucheru, is the health director for the Beaver First Nation in Alberta. Even though he's known Third World poverty himself, Gucheru is shocked at conditions on the reserve.

"I see a lot of sadness, especially when I go into homes," he tells me after a workshop comparing the experience of North American Indians with that of Black Americans. "I find that some of the homes on the reserve are very poorly constructed. Currently I'm getting phone calls because people have mould. I went to these homes and my heart was broken, because there were holes in the wall and in one house there were two bedrooms and seven people. I asked the owner how she survives in winter. I talked to the chief, and his situation is even worse, because he has a three-bedroom house with fourteen people living there. The chief is very self-sacrificing, and he doesn't abuse the money. There just isn't enough, because there are more people than there is money. They haven't done a proper census for ten to fifteen years, and funding is given out according to the population."

I ask Gucheru how the social conditions he sees on the Beaver reserve compare to what he grew up with in Kenya.

"In Africa, my father fought in the Mau Mau uprising, and he carries the trauma of colonialism. I told a workshop of residential school survivors that what is happening in Canada is also happening in Africa. Alcoholism is a big thing. My mom brewed beer for my dad, and I never saw my dad sober for one day. He could beat my mom any time of the day, even if she did nothing. I myself carry that with me, because I am the first born of nine children. Alcoholism is everywhere. It's easier for me, as a public health professional, to help people because I've seen it where I come from and can walk in their shoes and identify with them."

Frank Chee Waletto is a Navaho from New Mexico. He was a "code talker" who assisted the U.S. Marines during the Second World War, transmitting messages in Navaho that neither the Japanese nor the Germans could translate. Waletto, a frail man now in his seventies, receives a standing ovation from the delegates, many of whom know the importance of his work from the 2002 movie *Windtalkers*, starring Nicolas Cage and Adam Beach.

"We were a big help in the war effort," Waletto says to me, after the crowd of autograph-seekers clears off. "But prosperity hasn't come to the Navaho in the years since. My people don't have running water. Some don't have electricity. We still haul water for our home. Children are going to school but somehow are not progressing very much. Navaho economic development is very hard to start. Why? I don't know. Not much business comes on the reservation, and I would say more than 50 per cent of our people don't have jobs. We still raise some sheep, horses and cattle, and this is mostly what's helping us get along."

I ask Frank Waletto what social problems are prevalent in Navaho communities. It's a familiar story. "We're losing our young people to drugs and alcohol. What needs to be done is a lot of teaching, going back to the traditions. We're doing that, but it's slow. We're getting little support for economic development. The treaty that was made in 1868 obliges the U.S. government to educate our young and take care of our sick, but they're doing very little of that, because there are so many more of us. There are 300,000 Navaho, and as our population increases the government help doesn't increase proportionately."

While there is much talk over the week about the need for governments to increase services to Aboriginal communities, the central philosophy of Healing Our Spirit Worldwide is that Aboriginal people must take responsibility for their own actions. Each individual must become a role model for their families and their communities. Tom Porter, a Mohawk elder who lives near the Canada–U.S. border, entertains children during the conference, and then, at a morning plenary session, delights his adult audience with warmth and humour. His message stresses the importance of a good work ethic.

"If you're going to find happiness you have to unbutton your cuffs and push your sleeves up to your elbow and be ready to work and work hard and do it right," he says. "You do this so your family will survive and your children will not go hungry. Nobody likes lazy people. Always Grandma said, 'Get ready to help.' No matter where you go, pick up a broom and sweep up. Help them clean up. Even last night when they fed us, I wanted to go back into the kitchen to help with the dishes because I remembered what Grandma said. That's the old Indian way. Be helpful wherever you go, and that's my advice to everybody."

Porter's talk includes a special appeal to Aboriginal youth: "I want the young people to know that if you are troubled, if something is wrong, then look for us, the older ones, before you do anything foolish. Give us a chance to see if we can hold you and hug you, and maybe you'll change your mind, to stay and roll up your sleeves, too. Because very soon, if you do everything right, it's time to go. Our life is over and that's when we go, with great honour and dignity, not with suicides. So I send a message to stop that. Our Creator wants us to have peace, and the only way that we can have peace is if we respect and honour everything that the Creator made. When he made the Inuit he made them a certain way and he gave them songs, and we have heard how beautiful they are. When he made the Lakota he gave them certain songs and a certain way, and so it is in New Zealand and Australia. All over the world he made us to be like beautiful flowers. All over the world, all different colours, different shapes and different fragrances. Together those flowers, they never lose their identities, but when they're brought together, they make the most beautiful, awesome bouquet the universe can produce. And that's what you see gathered here today." Wild applause greets his words.

As the conference draws to a close, I ask Maggie Hodgson what quality has enabled her to realize the magnificent vision of this international healing movement.

"I think that the Creator has guided me in a lot of my decisions," she tells me. "I'd sure like to take credit for it, but ultimately I have grandfathers and grandmothers and God that guides me. The lessons that were given to me by my parents have also been very helpful. They told me that in order to do what I need to do, I must never, ever do it alone. Everything that has ever happened has been the result of the work of other people."

A few months after the Edmonton healing conference, Dr. Marjorie Hodgson would be made an Officer of the Order of Canada. It was another honour for a woman who has received many. The high school graduate has a couple of honorary university degrees and was among 1,000 women from around the world (ten were Canadian) nominated for the 2005 Nobel

Peace Prize. But the honours bestowed on her by her own people are the most meaningful. That is plain to everyone seated in the conference auditorium at the closing of Healing Our Spirit Worldwide. Hodgson's colleagues present her with a parting gift, since she will no longer be an active organizer. It's a carving of an eagle holding the earth within its wings. With it, Hodgson is given the title "vision keeper." A suitable title, since visions—and realizing them—are very much her thing.

But Maggie Hodgson, Rod Jeffries and the many other committed people in the Aboriginal healing movement have their fingers in a dike, holding back flood waters that could create horrendous tragedies for generations to come. If there is not greater support for their efforts, First Nations and Inuit communities may be engulfed in the tide of addiction and family violence that is causing widespread havoc for the next generation.

A Frightening Prognosis

DR. TED ROSALES IS A PEDIATRIC GENETICIST IN ST. John's, Newfoundland. He was one of the first specialists in Canada with the expertise to diagnose fetal alcohol spectrum disorder (FASD), a debilitating learning condition. An experience he had in 2001 so shocked Dr. Rosales that he has postponed his retirement to continue raising awareness of the problem in Aboriginal communities.

"If alcohol use during pregnancy is not stopped, the next generation will not have the brain capacity to appreciate their own culture as something they should be proud of," Rosales warns. "Unfortunately, I see this so many times. At the same time, I see the vision of young people who have not been alcohol-affected. They continue to do really good work, but without change they are going to be the minority, and they will not be able to continue this vision that they have."

Rosales, now sixty-nine, spends some of his free time poring over portraits of Aboriginal people in museums and history books, searching for evidence of FASD in the past. He looks closely at the upper lip, the nose and the space between the eyes. People brain-damaged by intrauterine exposure to alcohol have a thin upper lip, and their eyes tend to be closer together because the midface is elongated. Rosales can't find these facial features in the pictures he has examined. That's caused him to conclude that prior to the 1950s the condition, if it existed, was indiscernible in Aboriginal societies.

"I've never seen an FASD face in the old pictures," Rosales told me. "I'm certain it wasn't a problem for Aboriginal people in the past."

The brain is the first organ to develop in the womb, and our faces grow out of it. When a pregnant woman consumes alcohol, much of it remains in the placenta. A brain soaked in alcohol sustains damage. The face of an affected child reflects the extent of that damage, even before the child shows personality traits associated with FASD. The more subtle facial characteristics in milder cases of FASD are not enough for a complete diagnosis, but Rosales is convinced that even the smallest exposure to alcohol during gestation decreases the brain potential of the developing fetus.

In 2001, forty Innu children were airlifted from their communities in Labrador to St. John's because they were routinely inhaling gasoline fumes from plastic bags. Gas sniffing, or "huffing," as it's also known, had become so widespread by 2000 in Labrador's two Innu communities, Sheshatshiu and Utshimassit (Davis Inlet), that Innu leaders asked for intervention under the province's child protection legislation. The provincial government of Newfoundland and Labrador was at a loss to know what to do. To ensure they'd stop sniffing gasoline, the children were airlifted to St. John's and placed under lock and key in a decommissioned maternity hospital. The move was heavy-handed, but provincial authorities had no precedent for this emergency. A team headed by Rosales was asked to examine the children, who were closely supervised for four months.

Rosales and the other doctors first became aware of FASD when they could find no genetic explanation for the behavioural and learning problems in some of their young patients. "What we did was the best ever in terms of laboratory evaluation," says Rosales today. "We did all kinds of blood work, chromosome studies and cranial ultrasound, even MRI on some of them. We concluded that twenty-nine of these forty children had FASD."

The children called the kindly doctor, who is a native of the Philippines, "Dr. Miyagi" after a character in the *Karate Kid* movies. The situation was chaotic as Rosales made his daily rounds in the locked-down facility. It was not a good idea to confine so many children with FASD in a single space. The children were also traumatized by their confinement itself. They made closely supervised excursions to swimming pools, movies and the mall but had little interaction with the St. John's public. Their families were flown in from Labrador to visit them once.

According to the Canadian Paediatric Society, individuals with FASD have poor organizational skills, make poor choices and are unable to foresee the consequences of their actions. They are impulsive, show inappropriate behaviour because they can't read social cues, are excessively friendly and lack inhibition. This makes the children very difficult to parent, and it makes it hard for them to have a happy life. Rosales became fond of the children under his care. According to Rosales, the ringleader of widespread mischief at the Grace Hospital was a fourteen-year-old boy named J.B. Rich.

"He was the first one brave enough to call me Dr. Miyagi to my face," Rosales remembered with a smile. "You know, whatever came to his mind, he'd say. And if he thought of doing something, he went ahead and did it. He was always in the middle of the trouble."

Rosales poured heart and soul into a report that included not just diagnoses but also recommendations on ways to support the children with FASD throughout their lives. However, he told me, after some counselling and solvent abuse therapy, the children were sent back home and his report was set aside. Rosales next saw J.B. Rich three years later in a Labrador courtroom. The doctor sat and listened to the litany of petty crimes the boy had committed. He learned that J.B. had been in and out of the Goose Bay correctional centre, that his life was going nowhere but down. When it came time to take the stand in J.B.'s defence, Rosales lashed out at the officials who had let this happen.

"If they had done what I suggested, if he'd been given the community resources I said he'd need, this wouldn't have happened. I spelled it out. My recommendation was that all these children needed ongoing, lifelong resources and support. But my report never got any attention from the provincial or federal governments or the local community. It cost $6.5 million to do it. And the outcome was that it was shelved."

After testifying that day, Rosales went to lunch. He noticed J.B. sitting at a table by himself and went to join him.

"I asked how he was and whether he had a girlfriend and so forth," Rosales remembers. "He wasn't the same, not talkative at all. He was so changed. And I was really puzzled by that.

Looking back, I think that it was dawning on him. Everything that was going wrong, and why."

It was July 2004, and Rosales was scheduled to go on a family vacation. When he got back in August, he e-mailed J.B.'s legal aid lawyer. Rosales read down through the reply, which included comments the judge had made before sentencing J.B. to forty days of community service. The lawyer's final words shocked him: "Sad to say, he killed himself."

"J.B. hung himself shortly after the trial, and a few weeks later his brother Charlie did the same. Charlie also had FASD," Rosales told me during an interview in my home in the fall of 2006, his voice cracking. "I could have done more."

Rosales could not have acted as the "second brain" for J.B., though, any more than he could have for the other Innu children he diagnosed. As his recommendations outlined, all of them needed someone in their lives to play this crucial role.

"The second brain is essentially a caretaker, maybe the mother, foster mother or some relative who has a fair amount of knowledge about individuals with FASD," he explained. "This is somebody you can talk to and who can advise about FASD and how it applies to the particular individual. This extra brain may be a teacher in school, a social worker or even just a friend."

J.B. and Charlie Rich are buried beside one another in the graveyard in Natuashish. Their graves are marked with identical wooden crosses decorated with plastic flowers, rosary beads and their baseball caps. J.B. and Charlie are not the only young people from that 2001 airlift now dead from suicide. Dr. Rosales told me he believes there have been three more, at least. It's hard to know for sure, because no one is keeping track of these young people as he recommended.

"I almost gave up doing diagnoses for the courts," Rosales said. "What's the point of having people like J.B. hear they have FASD if they are not going to get services to help them? But I have to keep talking about it, because I want the courts, the judges, the social workers, the parents, the community members, the leaders to understand how serious and prevalent a problem this is. And I want it to stop. I want the children with FASD helped, and I want mothers helped so they will stop drinking."

He sees two ways to halt the spread of this condition: raising the standard of living in Aboriginal communities and launching a public health campaign on the scale of tobacco cessation programs in the South. He thinks such a campaign would work. After all, twenty-five years ago no one could have imagined banning smoking in bars and other public places.

"From a public health point of view, that's the only program I know that will work," Rosales said. "Whatever happens in the next fifty years, we will see the outcome. But unless things are changed now, I think the very existence of Aboriginal people as a culture, as a unique group of individuals, is really at stake."

Rosales developed this view after spending time in Nunatsiavut, the Labrador Inuit territory. One community there he believes has a rate of FASD damage in the 30 to 40 per cent range.

"That's after three generations of alcoholism," he said. "Given the same period of time, without drastic changes, I would assume that the population of individuals with brain damage from intrauterine alcohol will likely double, maybe more than double, in the next fifty years." Several murders and violent assaults in the community have already been committed by FASD–affected individuals.

Consumption of alcohol during pregnancy causes more birth defects than spina bifida (which stems from a nutritional deficiency) and Down syndrome (a genetic abnormality). FASD is sometimes mistakenly diagnosed as attention deficit hyperactivity disorder, mild autism or one of the other common learning and behavioural disorders among children. And the condition is not just a problem for Aboriginals. Dr. Rosales first saw babies damaged by prenatal alcohol exposure in rural Newfoundland.

"I went into a delivery room in Grand Falls," he recalled, "and the smell of alcohol was so powerful you'd think it was a brewery. The baby had been soaking in alcohol throughout the pregnancy."

In Canada, it is believed 10 babies in every 1,000 are born with FASD. In some Aboriginal communities an estimated 190 babies out of every 1,000 are affected.

"If we don't act now," Rosales told me, "we will end up with a lot of very brain-dysfunctional individuals in the future who will be making decisions for their community. Because they are the majority, things will really become very bleak for the community itself."

Rosales thinks Aboriginal people metabolize alcohol differently, making it more difficult for them to drink moderately. Activist Maggie Hodgson agrees, but as yet there's no scientific evidence to support this conclusion. Other experts say Aboriginal people are more prone to alcoholism because of the intergenerational trauma brought on by Canadian policies such as residential schools and the loss of traditional ways of life. Whatever the cause, both Rosales and Hodgson believe that zero tolerance for alcohol, not just among pregnant women but in whole communities, is necessary to prevent the widespread occurrence of FASD. Rosales also believes Aboriginal communities must be supported with increased health services and a higher standard of living. Yet instead of getting greater support, FASD prevention was one of five Aboriginal programs run by Health Canada that suffered budget cuts in 2006, despite a time of unprecedented prosperity in the country. The other four were tobacco cessation; the healthy mothers, healthy babies program, and programs aimed at suicide and diabetes prevention.

Ted Rosales had worked hard to make a difference. Among other initiatives, he served as a mentor to Mary Pia Benuen, an Innu nurse in the community of Sheshatshiu. In the summer of 2006, Benuen helped to organize a gathering of 286 Innu women at a camp in the Labrador wilderness. FASD was one of the issues the women talked about. A group of young girls put on a play that promoted abstinence from alcohol.

"One young girl played a pregnant teen who was being pressured by her peers to drink," Benuen told me. "She looked lonely for a while, and then her friends came around and supported her by stopping drinking themselves. It was very moving and got everybody talking."

Benuen is also an advocate for twenty-four children in Sheshatshiu between the ages of four and sixteen who have been diagnosed by Dr. Rosales with FASD. She makes sure the children get the support they need in school and at home. Benuen is upbeat about her job, but she wishes more Innu women were trained in the health care field. The Innu community of Natuashish does not have anyone to do the work Benuen is doing, nor do many other Aboriginal communities.

Rosales now travels across Newfoundland and Labrador at the invitation of health boards as a private consultant. He'd like to see the province do more to develop new experts, so that he can take the rest he deserves at this stage of his life. "This should really be a provincial program," he told me, "but to date the government has not come across with the funding needed."

BY CONTRAST, THE challenge of FASD is being treated with an unprecedented sense of urgency in Canada's western provinces and northern territories. In 2003 the Canada-Northwest FASD Task Force was created by the areas' health ministers. There is nothing similar for Ontario, Quebec or the Atlantic provinces, but the task force pools the resources that Alberta, Saskatchewan, Manitoba, British Columbia, Nunavut, Yukon and the Northwest Territories had been spending on their own to combat the problem. One of the world's leading experts, Dr. Sterling Clarren, has been hired by the task force as CEO and scientific director. Clarren, based at Vancouver's Centre for Community Child Health Research, moved to Canada from the United States because he was so impressed with the work being done here.

"Something happened here, a tipping point," he told me, "because the amount of FASD work going on in Canada is unique in the world."

Clarren's mission is to make sure that work is better coordinated and focussed on finding practical solutions. When he joined the task force, there were 170 government-funded FASD projects in northwest Canada alone, and a staggering 17,000 pamphlets, brochures and videos had been produced in the region.

"But it was not being done in an organized way," Clarren explained. "What's effective? If we want to be serious about prevention, we need to put our energies together to be thoughtful about how we do it."

Clarren began studying FASD in 1975 at the University of Washington, where his commitment became so widely known over the years that the author of a famous memoir on FASD sent the doctor his deceased son's brain to study. Michael Dorris's 1989 book, *The Broken Cord,* brought world attention to FASD. The book describes what Dorris learned about the condition from his adopted son Abel. Abel's intellectual and reasoning capacities were so seriously damaged he couldn't learn from experience and was unable to work without assistance. Sadly, he was killed by a hit and run driver shortly after the book was published.

As a result of the public interest generated by Dorris's book, Clarren and his colleagues founded the Fetal Alcohol Syndrome Information Service at the University of Washington. They wanted to warn pregnant women that alcohol consumed during the first trimester interferes with the organization of brain cells in the fetus; in the later months, alcohol affects areas in the brain related to memory, emotion and learning.

Today, Clarren is developing a health policy model on the treatment and prevention of FASD that he hopes will be applied across Canada. "The other provinces could join us, or the federal government could take control," he said. "In the end, I think this field needs a maximum of collaboration and cooperation and a minimum of competition. There is just so much work to do, so few resources and so little time to waste." Clarren's group has been funded until the end of 2008. By then, he hopes to have produced enough persuasive evidence to bring the other provinces and the federal government on board with an expanded budget and a renewed mandate.

About 1,100 children a year in northwestern Canada are tested for FASD, but Clarren said this is not enough to determine the full extent of the problem. He doesn't want Aboriginal societies stigmatized by FASD; his warning is for everyone. "Any society that drinks a lot puts their unborn at high risk," he told me when we spoke by telephone one Saturday afternoon in 2006. I'd sent him an e-mail and was surprised to find him at work on a weekend.

Michael Miltenberger, a former Northwest Territories minister of health, told me he believes 25 to 30 per cent of the Territories' 42,000 inhabitants are affected by the condition. "If we had alcohol stopped tomorrow, it would take the next eighty to ninety years for the system to clear itself of the troubles created by everyone who's damaged by alcohol," Miltenberger said. "Even if we were to do wonders tomorrow in terms of alcohol abuse, we have that segment of the population right from birth to age eighty who are damaged."

Sterling Clarren believes more effort needs to be placed on eradicating the conditions that cause women to drink even though they know it's wrong. He learned something valuable when he questioned alcohol-involved mothers in the United States.

"They have a universal experience with serious physical or sexual abuse," he told the Prairie Northern Conference on FASD in 2002. "They have mental health disorders. They have limited social supports, and half of them are brain-damaged themselves. I have never met a woman who drank through her pregnancy to hurt her baby. I don't think she exists."

TWENTY-THREE-YEAR-OLD Victoria Rich didn't drink during her pregnancy. I met and interviewed Rich in her home community of Natuashish in December 2005. She seemed fragile and delicate as we walked together from the community's health clinic, where Victoria works, to a nearby house for privacy. Once there, Victoria started to tell me the story of her life in halting English, her voice so soft it barely registered on my recording machine. She began by telling me how determined she was to give her son, Thomas, born in March 2006, a better life than she has had.

Rich was one of the children diagnosed with FASD by Dr. Ted Rosales. Apart from having been told she's affected, she has little other information. She just knows her condition is frightening. Victoria doesn't inhale gasoline now, nor does she drink alcohol. What has helped her most is her parents' sobriety. "My mother and my father, they stopped drinking almost two years now. I'm happy for them and I'm trying to get along with them," she says. Victoria is also determined to give Thomas a good start in life.

Thomas was just a month old when his nineteen-year-old uncle, Victoria's brother, committed suicide. Thomas's twenty-three-year-old father is a fixture in town, lurching at passersby on a lonely stretch of road while high on gasoline, sometimes landing himself in jail. If he doesn't accept help, Thomas's father may not survive to see Thomas start school. As it is now, he's prevented from having much contact with the baby.

The future of children such as Thomas Rich was compromised fifty years ago, write the evaluators of a major public health campaign to help the Innu. The federal government hired Institute of Environmental Research (IER) Planning, Research and Management Services and the Aboriginal Research Institute to evaluate the Labrador Innu Comprehensive Healing Strategy in 2003.

"In the 1960s, the self-sufficient lifestyle of the Labrador Innu came to an abrupt end with the settling of the two
communities of Davis Inlet and Sheshatshiu by the federal
government," say the evaluators. "Soon after . . . signs of addictive behaviour and social/family dysfunction became apparent.
Widespread alcohol use was prevalent by 1970."

Alcohol abuse was certainly prevalent when Victoria Rich
was born in 1986. Her birthplace, Davis Inlet, on the Labrador
coast, is an isolated "fly-in" community with some boat trans-
portation during the summer. It was a bad place to relocate
a hunting society. For most of the year, the Innu had no way
to get off the small island, which also lacked adequate fresh
water for a growing population. Despite the community's
isolation, it made international headlines a number of times
during Victoria's childhood, because of the terrible things that
happened there. When Victoria was six, a fire killed six pre-
school children who'd been left alone while their parents were
out drinking. A year later, Simeon Tshakapesh, a native con-
stable, took some video that was broadcast around the world;
it showed teens in Davis Inlet, high on gasoline, threatening
to kill themselves. Television reporters rushed to the town and
shot footage of its tumbledown shacks and garbage-strewn
streets. The publicity didn't change the living conditions in the
community, however. By the time Victoria was a teen, she was
inhaling gas fumes, too.

"I seen everything I didn't see before," she told me about her
fume-induced hallucinations. "Boys. They were small. Tiny-like.
They are on my eyes. But everybody told me there's nothing in
my eye. I told them I saw the Backstreet Boys, but they said it
was nothing. I was seeing it because I was sniffing gas."

Victoria quit school at twelve. The suffering in her community of 600, where most of the adults drank alcohol every day,

was excruciating. Some people tried to get help. In 1998 the band council hired a psychologist named Wayne Hammond, who had established a good reputation helping troubled native children in western Canada kick solvent abuse. He and the band council came up with some great ideas, but they received no government funding.

"Our plan was to build a stabilization home where kids who were really out of control could be brought and where we would work with the family as a whole," said Hammond, who now runs a company called Resiliency Canada. He was willing to move his own family from Alberta to Davis Inlet because of the emergency and had lined up other experts willing to do the same. "We also planned to develop alternate activities for kids in town so they'd have something else to do instead of hanging out at night. We were looking at a kind of caregiver model, where we would train people within the community to work with kids and families."

According to Hammond, bureaucrats in Ottawa were insensitive to the problem and refused to support the plan. Instead, in January 2001, after the Innu asked for emergency assistance, Victoria and thirty-nine other children were evacuated by air from Labrador. Efforts were made to heal them, but Victoria says she felt punished instead. "They took us to St. John's," she remembers, "and they locked us in a room for two or three hours. The gas sniffers, they break all the stuff. They break the toilet and the wall and they steal. They wanted to get out. I felt scared. I felt like I was in prison."

After their four-month stay in St. John's, the children were dispatched to treatment centres and foster homes across Canada, but they were not cured.

"I think we delayed the healing of the community by ten or fifteen years," Wayne Hammond says today, "because within

Health Canada and Indian and Northern Affairs there wasn't the courage to step out of the box."

Stepping out of the box would have meant providing addiction treatment in Davis Inlet, as the band council wished. Instead, government officials filled empty beds at treatment centres they were already funding in other parts of the country, many of which had no experience in helping child solvent abusers. It was a chaotic and frightening coming of age for Victoria and her friends. What she really needed was compassion for the damage done by her parents' alcoholism.

"Mom always went out drinking, and one day we were watching TV and my dad went out and sold it," she recalls. "They sell lots of stuff and we have nothing. We have no food or water. No wood. We burn clothes and paper, anything we had."

After the evacuation of their children, Innu leaders continued their campaign to get federal help for the addiction crisis that had their people in its grip. After a confrontation with former Prime Minister Jean Chretien at his home in Shawinigan in 2000, a major commitment was finally made to help solve Innu social problems. The Labrador Innu Comprehensive Healing Strategy, a multi-million dollar healing plan that is funded until 2010, is the result of this commitment.

One of the cornerstones of the healing strategy, the "relocation component," was used to move Davis Inlet residents to Natuashish, where there's clean drinking water, a state-of-the-art septic system, beautiful homes, a large, light-filled school, an arena, a band council building and, under construction, the long-awaited healing lodge and a shelter for victims of family violence. Relocation has helped bring hope to Victoria's people. The consultants who investigated the healing plan say, however, that having a nicer place to live is no guarantee of happiness.

"Physical construction and relocation is a qualified success, but social reconstruction is lacking," the IER report states. The Innu were supposed to be trained in carpentry and related trades as the new community was built, but that didn't happen. "Although seventy to ninety Innu were involved in the construction of Natuashish, only six have received sufficient training to continue to maintain the community without assistance."

Few, if any, Innu workers are involved in the construction now taking place in the community. Some middle-aged Innu are working at the nearby Voisey's Bay nickel mine, but most people Victoria Rich's age are not working. Victoria's mother, Mary Agathe Rich, is the receptionist at the Natuashish health clinic, which is staffed almost entirely by Innu. Sobriety is a condition of employment, and there's an air of optimism and purpose here. Victoria and her son, Thomas, visit frequently. Other frequent visitors come from the Nechi Institute in Alberta. The people from Nechi have not only offered the Mushuau Innu therapy for addiction and related issues, they have also trained community members to help themselves.

"Our friends stopped drinking after the Nechi program," Mary Agathe told me. "Now my husband and I are taking the programs, too."

Kathleen Benuen is an energetic woman who smiles and laughs easily, despite the almost daily crisis management she's engaged in as director of the Natuashish health commission. One of the commission's addiction therapists recently quit to return home to British Columbia. Benuen knows it won't be easy to find a replacement, but she's got to try. She has learned from her own experience with alcoholism (she's been sober for fourteen years) that it's important to take tough challenges one day at a time. Benuen, her community and the government bureaucrats share a common goal, which is eloquently summed up by one of the strategy's evaluators: "All agree that they want the Healing Strategy to succeed. All agree that the stakes are too high—with the future of the Innu children hanging in the balance—for the Healing Strategy to fail." Bureaucratic inefficiency and excessive control have seriously undermined the strategy already (see chapter 16), but the Innu believe they are on the road to recovery.

3

A Birthday Party

WHEN MAGGIE HODGSON AND HER COLLEAGUES BECAME activists in the 1970s, they warned the federal government it might one day be held legally liable if nothing was done to protect Aboriginal health from the addiction epidemic that was raging in Aboriginal communities across the country. The social collapse of many Aboriginal communities was already being reported in the mainstream press. One story that attracted a lot of attention was a mercury spill in the English-Wabigon river system that affected the northwestern Ontario reserves of Whitedog (Wabaseemoong) and Grassy Narrows (Asubpee-schoseewagong). But in her book, *A Poison Stronger than Love*, author Anestasia Shkilnyk linked the problems on the Ojibway reserve of Grassy Narrows to events that occurred before the mercury spill. To make way for a hydroelectric project, people had been moved to a location where they could no longer practise their traditional economy. The resultant alcoholism in their community became a poison even more destructive than mercury. In 1981, with the help of Aboriginal advisors such as Hodgson, the federal government established the National Native Alcohol and Drug Abuse Program (NNADAP). The acronym is pronounced "naydap" in most Aboriginal communities, where the program is very well known.

"We have the dubious distinction of being the only race of people in the country to have a government program geared to combat our alcoholism," Brian Maracle wrote wryly in his 1994 book, *Crazywater*. Yet by 2006 the program was being celebrated by the country's First Nations leadership with a birthday party as a source of great pride. NNADAP, today a division of Health Canada's First Nations and Inuit Health Branch, is a government program led and staffed largely by Aboriginals.

SIXTY-EIGHT-YEAR-OLD Barney Williams Jr. is a great supporter of NNADAP. As one of its first employees, he was invited to offer the opening and closing prayers at the NNADAP twenty-fifth anniversary banquet, held in Vancouver during the Assembly of First Nations annual general assembly in June 2006. The banquet was meant to celebrate the achievements of the veritable army of addiction workers employed by NNADAP in some of Canada's most troubled and isolated places, providing counselling, education and prevention programs. There are 700 community workers and another 700 employees at the program's fifty-six treatment centres, including those who work at ten centres helping youths who abuse solvents. Many people are being healed, but every year more young Aboriginals get sucked into the quagmire of addiction. Some community leaders are still not getting the message. That's probably because the message is not always clear.

By the time of the banquet, Williams had given up his cer-emonial post as the Tla-o-qui-aht First Nation's most respected Beach Keeper. His job was to greet visitors who arrived by sea and make sure they were comfortably housed and fed on the reserve. (Tla-o-qui-aht is located in Pacific Rim National Park near Tofino, British Columbia.) Williams left the reserve because he believes his people have stopped listening to the sea. He moved to a non-Aboriginal community called Parks-ville, on Vancouver Island, because he grew tired of witnessing the alcohol and drug abuse in his community. His frustration began when, as Tla-o-qui-aht chief, his efforts to stop the flow of alcohol and drugs onto the reserve were not supported.

I was lucky enough to be seated beside Williams at the NNADAP banquet, where I had been asked to talk about my research. He told me his inspiring yet troubling story.

"I tried to get council to pass a bylaw requiring people to be sober for two years before they could run for band council," Williams said, "but I got no support. No one wanted to support my plan to hold a public march opposing the bootleggers and pushers, either."

Williams was once an addict himself. Forty-three years ago, the sound of the sea helped to restore his life.

"I remember my first day of sobriety so clearly," he said. "I was sitting on a beach and heard the waves rolling back and forth. I kept thinking, I've missed out on so much. And then I began to cry, because I found the sound so beautiful and real-ized how close I came to never hearing it again."

Williams had lost his ability to hear the sea when he was sexually abused at residential school. He began drinking in his teens, but he stopped with help from his grandfather, who taught the young man his language and culture. Williams was recently compensated for the abuse at residential school, and he used that money to buy his new home off the reserve.

Tough measures are needed to wrestle the drug and alcohol problems in Tla-o-qui-aht, Williams told me. Before he left the reserve in 2005 he hired a young woman to be the local NNADAP worker. He believed she was already making a difference.

"She works seven days a week supporting families and managed to get fourteen people into treatment. Most of them are still sober," he said.

NNADAP has been credited with reducing alcohol abuse rates in First Nations communities across Canada from highs of 95 per cent, when Barney Williams was a young man, to half that today. In fact, a higher number of Aboriginal people (34 per cent) abstain completely from alcohol than do other Canadians (21 per cent). Williams and many others in the NNADAP program want to see the number of Aboriginal people abstaining from alcohol grow to 100 per cent. They believe only total abstinence from alcohol can solve their communities' social problems. That's because most of the Aboriginal people who do drink alcohol consume five or more alcoholic beverages at a time: the definition of binge drinking. There's a similar statistic among Canadian young people—39 per cent of them binge drink—but for non-Aboriginals that number drops off to 14 per cent by the time they hit middle age. There is no commensurate drop in the Aboriginal population; those who start binge drinking in their teens tend to keep it up. Saskatchewan sociologist Richard Thatcher, author of the book *Fighting Firewater Fictions*, says there's no physiological reason some Aboriginal people drink too much. The causes are social, he believes. The conditions for sobriety are absent from many Aboriginal communities.

"The very fact of trying to secure an education and employment, working, establishing a sober and supportive network of friends and acquaintances, working rationally and lovingly through spousal conflicts, fulfilling family obligations, engaging in wholesome recreational activities and contributing altruistically to community affairs are the best antidotes to addiction," Thatcher writes.

Creating such ideal conditions for societies that have been as marginalized as Canada's First Nations and Inuit is easier said than done. While waiting for the trauma to heal, and for social conditions to improve, Barney Williams and many like him believe the only way forward is to promote total abstinence from alcohol. It's a contentious issue. The merits of total abstinence versus harm reduction, another approach to addiction, were raised at the NNADAP banquet. Williams was suspicious at first when the room was slow to fill up.

"See," he said to me, "our members have been out partying. They're not concerned about our social problems."

But he was wrong. The invitations to the banquet had directed people to the wrong room, and by the time Williams rose to pray, most of the tables had been filled. Artist Roy Henry Vickers, whose father is of Tsimshian and Heiltsuk ancestry, had created a commemorative print for the occasion, and a copy was presented to each of the NNADAP workers invited to the banquet. The print, called "Open Hands," shows an intricate weave of hands reaching out to help one another. Vickers has been active in helping his people recover from alcohol addiction, and he knows how important this work is.

Geraldine Kelly, a Micmac from Conne River, Newfoundland, spoke after accepting her gift. Kelly told the assembled group that she began to work for NNADAP after her father died in a drunk driving accident. She's been preaching the virtues of abstinence from alcohol ever since. "I know from my experience that this program saves lives," she said. "And I hope it continues for another twenty-five years."

Richard Jock, the Assembly of First Nations chief executive officer, told diners that NNADAP is one of Health Canada's most comprehensive public health programs, and the first program delivered largely by Aboriginal employees. "The fact the program still exists, twenty-five years later, is a tribute to the First Nations and Inuit people," Jock said.

Then Bill Erasmus, regional chief of the Northwest Territories, rose to speak, describing the merits of harm reduction.

"We never learned how to be social drinkers," Erasmus told the assembled group. "We have to understand the whole issue of addiction. If people want to drink, they'll find a way to drink. Prohibition doesn't work. Rather than prohibition, children need to learn that alcohol is not a bad thing in and of itself. It's a medicine. It's a poison when you abuse it."

Barney Williams shook his head at this. He believes it's naive to think promoting social drinking can stop the destruction alcohol is causing in Aboriginal communities. "If they had served alcohol at this meal tonight," he told me, "I would have been deeply offended. I really believe that if we're going to beat this we have to take a hard stand."

The different positions represented by Erasmus and Williams are at the core of an ongoing debate. Harm reduction promotes public education about the safe use of alcohol and drugs. It also promotes measures to limit the harm these substances do to users and to the public when they're abused. NNADAP was founded on different principles, ones that are intolerant of any alcohol or drug use. It is based on the Alcoholics Anonymous (AA) model of addiction, which recognizes

alcoholism as a disease to which some people are more suscep-
tible than others.

Sociologist Richard Thatcher believes the AA model is
outmoded and actually slows addiction recovery by requiring
total abstinence. Harm reduction encourages people to heal
by cutting their consumption instead. Thatcher agrees with
Bill Erasmus that NNADAP would be better off promoting
programs that teach people to control the amount of alcohol
they consume rather than telling them to avoid alcohol completely. Thatcher feels Aboriginal addiction needs to be fought
on another front, through government policy. "Creating hope
through education, training, the family and economic development must be viewed as the most effective addictions and
problem drinking prevention strategy," he writes.

Sharon Clarke has been following this debate closely.
Clarke served for six years as executive director of the National
Native Addictions Partnership Foundation, an organization
founded to improve NNADAP following a review of the program's work in 1998. She is a Saskatchewan Cree who has
also worked within Health Canada and NNADAP. She often
collaborates with Richard Thatcher on research projects, but
she doesn't share all of his views. Clarke says despite medical
evidence that Aboriginal people do not have a genetic predis-
position to alcoholism, her own experience proves otherwise.
She stopped drinking when she noticed she easily lost control
after a few drinks.

"Once I started drinking I couldn't stop," she told me over
coffee at the Healing Our Spirit conference. "We've struggled
with the harm reduction concept and a moderate drinking
style in our organization, but for us right now abstinence has
worked very well."

Treatment centres run by NNADAP have the same rate of success as non-Aboriginal treatment centres, and they are accredited by the same organization, the Canadian Council on Health Services Accreditation. NNADAP centres differ by emphasizing the importance of Aboriginal spiritual and cultural values, coupled with abstinence. Like NNADAP and the National Native Addictions Partnership Foundation, the Assembly of First Nations also has a total abstinence policy. "Alcohol-free is the only way to go," Richard Jock of the AFN told me. "If you're an organization, your event should be alcohol free, and your organization should not pay for alcohol at any hospitality function."

This is a change from the past. Sharon Clarke remembers a time when Aboriginal political leaders and even addiction workers consumed alcohol at gatherings. She doesn't see that today, and she says the abstinence movement is growing. Williams and the leaders of NNADAP have a simple message for Aboriginal people: alcohol and drugs must be kept out of their communities completely. Abstinence is the only way to guarantee the survival of Aboriginal societies, they say, especially now that more is known about the effects of prenatal exposure to alcohol.

Richard Thatcher's prescription for a happy life—jobs, good schools, lots of recreation programs, secure families—won't happen on reserves or in Metis and Inuit communities until governments build hope by investing in better social conditions and Aboriginal people take greater responsibility for their own behaviour. Barney Williams has done that. Today he volunteers as a counsellor for people who attended residential schools and didn't learn how to parent or build loving relationships. He tells the people he talks to they must exercise responsibility by abstaining from alcohol and drugs as a first step. At the NNADAP banquet, he had a few final comments to make before offering his closing prayer.

"Addiction is the worst thing that has ever happened to our people," he told the gathering. "Every person that becomes sober has a snowball effect on others. Work hard. Tell the people who are still drinking to stop. There are better things in life."

4

A Crippling Affliction

ONE MORNING IN SEPTEMBER 2006 I RECEIVED A call from anthropologist Peter Armitage, telling me that Peter Penashue's first cousin from Sheshatshiu was in hospital in St. John's. Fifty-two-year-old Greg Penashue was in a bad way when I went to visit him. It was a shock to see him lying in the hospital bed, hooked up to supports for breathing, feeding and other vital functions while a nurse kept watch over him.

I'd met Greg in the late 1970s while reporting on life in Sheshatshiu for CBC Television. He was one of the first "school-educated" Innu, an English speaker who was among half a dozen young men sharing the political leadership of the community at that time. He served as an elected leader with the Innu Nation for ten years, and on the side he sang with a popular group of Labrador musicians called the Flummies.

More recently, I had produced a film for CBC Television and The Rooms, the Newfoundland and Labrador provincial museum, about Greg's father, Pien, who was making a traditional canoe from scratch. The seventy-six-year-old man cut down a white spruce tree, then split the wood himself with a small axe. He made strips for the canoe frame, shaving them paper thin so they'd become supple when soaked in hot water and more easily bent into shape by his knees. The canoe was then covered with canvas, painted and put on display at the provincial museum. Although he was nearly blind when he did all of this, Pien Penashue created a perfectly proportioned canoe, as he'd done countless times in his lifetime.

Pien Penashue is a remarkable man in other ways. I saw him put a judge and an audience of RCMP officers to shame during proceedings at the Goose Bay courthouse in 1989. Pien had been arrested for trespassing on the runways at CFB Goose Bay during a protest against low-level jet flights over Innu traditional territory. "Who gave you authority over me?" he asked the judge through an interpreter. "This place where you have built this building used to be a good place to pick berries. I have walked all over the land. You see the land from airplanes. I have walked it all, and I see what damage you are doing on the ground. We had no need of judges and police before you came."

Now Pien's son Greg was very ill, reduced to speaking in a raspy whisper, his body surprisingly thin on his large frame. The cause? A stroke brought on by a prolonged binge-drinking session. Greg later told me he had been drinking like this while his wife, Theresa, was working as a housekeeper at the Voisey's Bay nickel mine, a fly-in camp several hundred kilometres north of Sheshatshiu. She was gone for weeks at a time, and loneliness for Theresa had led him to drink out of control.

Greg was released from hospital after several weeks in care and returned to Sheshatshiu. He now relies on a wheelchair, though, and his life is forever altered. I visited him at his home a few months after his stroke. Greg used to pride himself on being a moderate drinker, he told me, but as he got older this changed.

"I overdid it this time, I think," he said. "Whenever I got up I drank, again and again. There are pills I'm supposed to take for high blood pressure, and I didn't take them. I didn't eat. I just drank. I usually drank a dozen beer, passed out, and the next morning drank again. That's it."

He had quit drinking since the stroke but missed the camaraderie of his former drinking buddies. "I used to have a lot of friends back then," he told me. "Younger friends. My nephews and my wife's brothers and sisters and my cousins, and I haven't seen them now, no. I guess it's because I haven't drunk for five months now. I haven't touched a beer. I don't smoke. It's kind of confusing in one way, because you used to have these people with you when you were drinking, and now you don't have them. They're all gone now. They're around here, but they're still drinking and never come to see me."

Children in the community are badly affected by the amount of drinking that goes on, Greg told me, and he's even more aware of it now that he can't leave the house. "We live close to the beach. Most of the kids who live around here have no one to look after them, so we usually look after more kids here on the weekend. The parents aren't home, they're out drinking. The sad thing is, what do you do? People who don't drink still go out anyway, because they're gambling. Kids we know, they're all by themselves at the house next door because their parents gamble. They go to bingo, they go to clubs to play the slot machines. The children, they're ten and less. A week before I got out of hospital there was a house fire here. The parents were up in Goose Bay and the kids were at home. The children might have died, like what happened in Utshimassit [Davis Inlet, where six children under the age of ten died in a house fire]. I guess they must have spotted it and run out."

With Greg's permission, I tried to get his health records, but for some reason the Labrador-Grenfell Health Authority blocked my request. The doctor in Sheshatshiu supported my inquiry, because he believed other heavy drinkers in the community could benefit from knowing what happened to Greg. Theresa Penashue must now maintain a vigil over her disabled husband. She has quit her job to share his confinement, and their lives are less productive than they used to be. Greg has become a kind of armchair observer of the life of his people, and he is often nostalgic about the past. "If you're in the country you have to work hard," he told me. "Nobody works hard anymore. Like when I was raising my family I used to use wood heat. I'd be in the woods cutting wood, and there used to be a big lump for putting wood on my shoulder, to carry it. There's even an Innu word for the big lump we grew on our necks for carrying canoes."

Greg told me boredom drives some of his family members, who also live in Sheshatshiu, to drink. News of a party is one of the few things that breaks the monotony of their everyday lives. "They don't work. All they do is watch TV. Violent movies, scary movies. I have a daughter who does drugs, marijuana, and I usually give her the money. I don't like what she does with the money, but I give it to her anyway. Why? I don't know. She's my daughter, that's it. The same thing goes for my mom and dad. They don't drink at all, they haven't for as long as I remember. But one of my brothers drinks. And where does he get that money from? My mom and dad. That means my mom and dad are giving him money to drink."

There's a high cost to the non-drinkers in troubled communities of indulging their loved ones, yet it's hard not to "enable." A friend of mine in her sixties, Tshaukuesh Penashue, asked one of her sons to leave the house because his heavy drinking was disturbing her sleep and her peace of mind. But when she discovered he was sleeping in the crawl space under the church in Sheshatshiu, and basically living outside, she couldn't bear it. She invited him back home again. Housing shortages in Aboriginal communities mean there are few options but to shelter a drinking family member in your home. That can be a frightening experience.

"Most of the people I know are scared of their son or grandson," Greg Penashue told me. "We even have a peace bond here for when our daughter drinks. She gets rough when she drinks. She cooks at night, and we can't sleep because she's drinking and we're worried what might happen."

According to the results of the 2002–2003 Regional Longitudinal Health Survey—the only First Nations–governed health study in Canada—there are more alcohol abstainers in Aboriginal communities than there are in the general Canadian population. That's the good news. The bad news is that there are twice as many problem Aboriginal drinkers than there are in the general population. No one can explain precisely why this is so. Sociologist Richard Thatcher, who also publishes a magazine on Aboriginal health issues called *Circle Talk*, believes this "all or nothing" style of drinking is a carryover from frontier times. The alcohol that Aboriginals received in exchange for furs would be consumed all at once, so that the nomadic Indians and Inuit could continue on their travels. Frontier workers also tended to be binge drinkers, because they worked in isolated places and had no family responsibilities.

Thatcher believes Aboriginals picked up binge drinking from these early European contacts. There are many reasons it's still widely practised, he explained.

"The evidence points to a bio-psycho-social model of substance abuse in which there are many causes," Thatcher outlined in an e-mail he sent me. "The Firewater Complex concept is about an ideology that internalizes a permanent sense of victimization within the Aboriginal population... and keeps them in a quasi-institutionalized state of being with the help of a host of police, lawyers, probation and parole officers, and mental health and substance abuse workers. The best prevention literature calls for fundamental anti-poverty programming and argues for careful identification of the problem drinker's motivation for change." In Thatcher's opinion, "A treatment goal oriented to harm reduction rather than abstinence is essential for the unmotivated and many of the most heavily dependent, extremely unhealthy drinkers. Also, when there are no serious employment opportunities at the other end of treatment, then even the best of treatment outcomes are gradually compromised. So, the best treatment for substance abuse involves socio-economic development linked to personal empowerment."

If moderate drinking *is* possible, it may take some time for the practice to trickle down to the community level, where there's often a belief that to drink is to drink crazily, as though there is no tomorrow. Jobs alone may not be the answer.

Tshaukuesh Penashue explained to me what happened to her grandson's first pay cheque from the Voisey's Bay nickel mine. "He asked me to go with him to buy groceries," she said, "and he was very happy. But then all the other money he earned was spent on drugs and alcohol." When I suggested her grandson start saving to buy a house, Tshaukuesh replied incredulously, "You think buying a house will make him happy?" He'd be happier if he was hunting, she believes, and if he spent more time in the natural environment. "When I leave the community and go in my tent, I am very happy," she told me. "I sleep good, and when I get an animal to eat, I know I'm going to eat good."

In whatever way sobriety is achieved, there's no doubt that a beautiful change comes into the lives of Aboriginal people lucky enough to escape the grip of binge drinking. Outside Sheshatshiu's medical clinic I bumped into Michel Rich, an Innu entrepreneur. When I explained my research, he was eager to tell me his own story.

"I've been sober for the past thirteen years. My last beer was December 15, 1995. The first two years was hard. At the time I really believed I could do it, and being an alcoholic was really, really a poor life for me. I guess what motivated me was when I done bodily harm on my missus, and I realized that I was abusing the woman I love. So then I started looking in the mirror and saw two Michel Riches, one in the mirror and one in my body. Looking in the mirror I was looking at the reflection of myself. And I talked to the mirror. I said, 'Michel, you're making my life really miserable. You turned me into an alcoholic. You turned me into a criminal, and that got to stop.' So I hit the mirror, and when I hit the mirror the pain bounced back on my body, I guess, and I feel it and then I realized my problem was *me*. I had to fight myself inside to start a new life. Since my sobriety I took my family to Florida to enjoy life, and I'm just trying to catch up the life I messed up. So as of right now I'm in easy life, easy living. I got no problems with alcohol, and I got no problems with friends of mine when they drink.

I can enjoy them with their beer and my coffee on the side and laugh. In the meantime, they don't push me into drinking. They just say, how can you do it? I said, 'It's easy, it's like quitting smoking.' But I can't quit smoking; it's really, really hard for me. So, as of now I enjoy my life and the last thirteen years of my sobriety. Time flies. When I was drinking I thought I was having a good time."

Michel's parents drank, and he spent most of his childhood in foster care. Now he and his wife are raising a little girl they adopted to keep them busy and happy since their own three children have grown up and left home.

Every sober person in an Aboriginal community is an important role model, and a turning point is reached when the number of non-drinkers begins to outnumber those who are still drinking. Those involved in self-destructive behaviour begin to see the possibilities for happier lives. Building this momentum for change is a crucial part of the solution for Aboriginal communities.

A Family's Triumph
over Addiction

SIXTY-THREE-YEAR-OLD FRANCIS PENASHUE LEANED
forward, watching the pomp and circumstance from the raised
box seat usually reserved for Newfoundland and Labrador's
lieutenant-governor. I waved to him from across the auditorium of the St. John's Arts and Culture Centre. He waved back,
then resumed his search for his wife on the stage below. Tshaukuesh (Elizabeth Penashue) was about to receive an honorary
degree from Memorial University. Tshaukuesh was seated
behind the dignitaries, who included the university chancel-
lor, former politician John Crosbie. Her son Jack was seated
beside her, there to translate her acceptance speech into English. Francis turned towards his eldest daughter and whispered
something that made her laugh. Five of his nine children had
come to St. John's from Sheshatshiu for the ceremony.

Tshaukuesh had added some cultural touches to her academic dress—moccasins and a colourful red and navy Innu

cap. Jack wore his University of Regina graduation gown. This was a proud moment for a family that has suffered every social ill known to Aboriginals.

It might never have happened had the Penashues not been willing to go to a place where alcoholism was the only thing they had in common with others, and where they had to trust another Roman Catholic priest. Priests are one reason the Penashue family got broken in the first place. Time and again Roman Catholic priests betrayed this family's trust. And yet a Roman Catholic priest pulled the Penashues out, one by one, from the dark hole into which they were sinking. Jack Penashue was filled with so much rage when he first saw a priest at the Brentwood Recovery Home for alcoholics in Windsor, Ontario, he thought he was going to kill him. But Jack wasn't the first Penashue to seek help at Brentwood. It was Peter, the eldest. He was twenty-six in 1991.

"I woke up one morning, it was my son's sixth birthday." Peter told me. "I was so sick, really hungover, and my wife had left me. All I could think was, how am I going to get her back and where am I going to find money to buy my son a present? I was really about as far down as you can get."

Peter jolted into action that day because he knew he was walking in his father's unsteady footsteps. Throughout childhood Peter had been the fixer, the one who tried to keep his siblings and his mother safe while his father drank.

I first met Peter Penashue in 1982, when he was seventeen. He and another Innu teen, Edward Nuna, boarded at my home in St. John's for ten months while attending high school. During that time, Peter received a letter from his brother Gervais, asking him to come home.

"Dad is drunk. He's beating up the house, and our mother. The stove is broke. There's no food or heat," Gervais wrote.

Peter, because he was the eldest, felt obliged to go, even though it would mean quitting school. I encouraged him to call his mother first. As I suspected, she wanted him to stay in school. I thought of a way to help. Peter received a small living allowance while he lived with me, and an advance on that would help his mother fix the stove and buy food. Peter only truly relaxed when he learned his family would be spending several months in their tent that winter, in the bush, where his father would no longer be drinking but instead providing for his family in the way he knew best.

In the days leading up to Christmas that year, an Innu man who was in St. John's on business knocked on my door and presented me with a package. "From Tshaukuesh," he said. Inside was a pair of caribou skin moccasins that fit my feet like a glove. Peter told me his mother had asked him to trace my shoes on a piece of brown paper and mail it to her for the moccasin pattern. I marvelled that she could have been so thoughtful while living under such tremendous stress, raising nine children in great difficulty.

Apinam Pone lived for moments like the one that brought twenty-six-year-old Peter Penashue to his door. At that time, Pone ran Sheshatshiu's National Native Alcohol and Drug Abuse Program. He had received help from the Brentwood Recovery Home himself when he lived in Windsor. Pone came triumphantly back to Sheshatshiu in the 1980s, sober and eager to run the "alcohol centre," as it's known, referring people in his community to treatment programs, running AA meetings and showing by example what sobriety has to offer.

"I wanted to go to Brentwood because that's where Apinam got sober," Peter recalled. "They didn't have a bed for me, so I begged Apinam to get me out of Sheshatshiu before the weekend. I knew I'd fall back into the drinking scene if I didn't go right away, and who knows how long I might have stayed like that and what more damage I'd do?"

Pone and the staff at Brentwood know there's only a small window to pull addicts through when they look for help. If the window isn't open, it may be years before someone will try again. Peter Penashue was in by the weekend. He returned from Brentwood sober and has stayed sober ever since, serving for a time as president of the Innu Nation, and now as vice president. He inspired other members of the family to get help, starting first with his father.

Francis Penashue was the only child of Kanituakuet, one of Sheshatshiu's most respected hunters. Kanituakuet was a man who never drank, never stopped believing and practising the Innu religion (although he adapted some Catholic beliefs), but he was also a man who didn't keep his son close enough to him after his wife's premature death. In the 1950s, when Francis was a boy, the Innu people still travelled nomadically, coming to Sheshatshiu only during the summer months. A priest persuaded Kanituakuet that Francis would be better off going to school than hunting for months at a time with his father. Francis stayed with the priest in Sheshatshiu. Once the priest disciplined him so harshly he couldn't use his right hand for a month. A few years later, Francis was sent to Mount Cashel Orphanage in St. John's to finish his English education. There he and another Innu boy hid in a closet when they got homesick and whispered together in their own language. The orphanage was closed in 1989 after its horrendous legacy of clerical sexual abuse became a national scandal and has since been demolished.

By the priest's reckoning Francis was a success. The boy had become an English speaker ready to help his people deal with the culture that surrounded them after they gave up their nomadism to live in houses built for them in Sheshatshiu in 1963. Francis became the band council chief, a concept foreign to the Innu then. Traditional Innu leadership was more organic; it was accorded to the most successful hunter, not the person who garnered the most votes. It was during this time that Francis began to binge drink to cope with stress and rage. Alcohol released so much anger inside him that his wife and children scattered for cover wherever they could find shelter in the community.

"Sometimes people turned us away," Tshaukuesh remembered, "because they were afraid of Francis."

Tshaukuesh drank too in the early years of her marriage. She stopped when her husband's violence escalated and she needed sobriety to stay alive. A younger priest offered to shelter her boys when their father was drunk. She didn't find out until years later how the priest had picked them off one by one, seeking sexual favours, terrifying them to get what he wanted.

"I'd hear him coming and would pretend I was asleep, or I'd lock myself into the bathroom. Then I'd feel guilty because he would take one of my younger brothers," Jack Penashue remembered.

This living nightmare led Jack down a self-destructive path that began with binge drinking during his teen years in the early 1980s and ended with frequent suicide attempts. "I drank Javex once, I hated myself so much," he told me. "I cut my wrists, took pills, even tried to shoot myself a couple of times. But people kept rescuing me."

As recently as 1988, a priest betrayed the Penashue family once again by seducing one of the younger boys. The priest had won trust in the community by going on a hunger strike to publicize an Innu political cause. It's remarkable that only three years later, Peter was able to trust another priest to cure his alcoholism. But he was desperate.

The priest he trusted was Father Paul Charbonneau, who founded the Brentwood Recovery Home in 1964 and has kept it running ever since. Charbonneau is a short, powerful-looking man, even now at eighty-five. He learned how to help addicts because he wanted to help their children. He was the child of addicts himself, and he knows the suffering it involves.

I travelled to Windsor in January 2006 to see what it is about the Brentwood program that helps problem drinkers like the Penashues. By then Father Charbonneau had cut back his visits to the centre to one day a week, but he agreed to meet me there.

"The children of addicts live in fear," he told me, seated behind a large desk in his office. "When I first started out as a young priest in my parish, I could tell in grades four, five, six: these kids come from an alcoholic home. You'd see them, their faces, their eyes. They'd be almost like dead inside. They wouldn't be alive at school. They'd be someplace else, afraid to go home. The whole atmosphere in an alcoholic home is generally one of terror, one of physical abuse, often sexual abuse. It's just horrible."

When Charbonneau began his work forty-four years ago, the Brentwood Recovery Home was a two-storey house in the centre of town. Today it's a series of sprawling buildings on the city's outskirts that, ironically, had once housed a nightclub and casino complex. It's a busy place that helps a hundred or more addicts at a time. There's no receptionist to greet visitors in the large lobby; this is a stripped-down place without the frills or concern for privacy that characterize other addiction centres. Former clients, or "alumni" as Brentwood's recovered addicts are called, come and go, looking for assistance in avoiding a relapse or a way to help newcomers. The alumni provide talk therapy, the main catalyst used here to change peoples' destructive behaviour.

"It's consciousness-raising," explained Don Russell, the centre's executive director. "It's the talking about the shame and the hurt that helps. We're not talking about how much booze or drugs we've had or used. That's only 5 per cent of the problem."

After persuasion from Peter, Francis Penashue went to Brentwood to get help for his alcoholism in 1993. He was deep in denial about how his drinking had adversely affected his family. But one of the Brentwood alumni, a former alcoholic, knew what was needed to get through to Francis.

"This man used to ask me, do you love your children?" Francis recalled during a conversation we had in his Sheshatshiu kitchen three years ago. "I said yes. And he said, no, you do not. He said I was never at any of my children's birthday parties, but I said I always was."

The man continued to confront Francis whenever they were in a group together. "He said, Francis, when the birthday was going on, were you there with friends? And I said yes. What he meant was, when my son had a birthday I used to get in a few dozen beers and call my friends and have a party to celebrate my son. That was mean, because I was not there. I had a party for myself and my friends. We frightened the children."

After three months of talking and listening to other addicts in this way, Penashue was able to empathize for the first time with his wife and children, something he could never do in the depth of his addiction. He was lucky to be able to leave Brentwood sober after such a short time; for many other addicts, it takes much longer. Today he's a gentle, loving husband and father who assists his wife, now also an important community leader. In the past, he told me, he'd have been consumed by jealousy to see her in this role.

Father Paul Charbonneau believes there's emotional trauma in an addict's childhood that damages his or her ability to trust anyone, especially for emotional needs. Addicts learn to satisfy themselves, pursuing gratification through alcohol, drugs, gambling, food or sex.

"They don't trust anybody because they hate honesty," the priest says. "They don't live by it and they just feel everybody is the enemy, even the wife and so on. They almost become evil, because they can't experience love. That's my definition. Our inability to let people in because we can't trust, and therefore our inability to love or to give love or to accept love. That's what an addict is."

"Many children of addicts go on drugs or booze to kill some of the pain," Father Charbonneau continues. "They join groups of people that do the same. They feel a little secure in a group since they can't really feel secure or at peace in their own family." This may help to explain the cycle of addiction in traumatized Aboriginal communities and the growing popularity of gangs among Aboriginal youth.

Most of Brentwood's clients are non-Aboriginal, since many Aboriginal people prefer treatment centres with a program that incorporates their spiritual and traditional beliefs. Father Charbonneau, however, sees value in getting Aboriginal and non-Aboriginal clients to work through their problems together.

"If they're still blaming the white man or the government, then they're into self-pity and they won't make that breakthrough," he says. "But when they're involved with the white person in recovery, then they have to trust this one and trust that one. They can make the breakthrough individually and as part of a group, which is so basic to being spiritual. Self-pity, blaming others, is really what alcoholism is all about."

It's too bad so much of Charbonneau and Russell's time today, and that of their staff, is spent fundraising to keep the centre going. The service provided at Brentwood and the formula of using former addicts (as well as professionals) to counsel newcomers really seem to work. Brentwood receives some funding from the government of Ontario and from Health Canada but would welcome more. Don Russell would like the federal government to fund ten beds a year at Brentwood specifically for Aboriginal clients. At present, many people go there because they've heard of the centre's success by word of mouth.

Francis and Tshaukuesh Penashue are grateful for Charbonneau's work. They worry about a son and a grandson who still binge drink, however. They hope the two will soon decide to seek help as they did. In the meantime, on that day in St. John's, there's a lot to celebrate. Tshaukuesh was being honoured for her environmental activism and her commitment to passing on Innu culture and in March 2008 she received a National Aboriginal Achievement Award for her effort. Tshaukuesh believes the cure for her people's social problems is for Innu of all ages to spend as much time as possible on the land. The active fifty-nine-year-old spends months each year leading long walks (which require setting up and dismantling tents every day), hunting, fishing and organizing canoe trips on the Churchill River, which she dearly hopes will not suffer any more damage from hydroelectric development.

Dr. Laurence Kirmayer, a cultural psychiatrist at McGill University, has coined the term "ecocentric" to refer to Aboriginal people; he says their alienation from the land due to industrial projects such as dams, logging and mines creates psychological problems that contribute towards the use and abuse of alcohol, drugs and gambling as a way of coping.

Tshaukuesh would share Kirmayer's view, and her speech at convocation certainly showed her to be "ecocentric" in this way. "I am very grateful that I am being given honours as I am a voice of people," she told the assembled group. "I am also a voice of the animals. I am also a voice for the environment. I am a voice of the people who cannot speak for themselves. I have a lot of relatives who are not able to present themselves. I fight for the injustice of what is happening to the environment, what is happening to the animals. You are probably aware that the Innu people are in crisis in our communities. And you are probably also aware of the suicides and the issues within our communities. The reasons we do these things are because we need to live the way we were always taught, to live among the land, among the environment and the animals. That is how we were raised to live. And if we start abusing the environment, then we start abusing the people who live on that land."

After convocation ended and all the pictures were taken, I was asked to join the Penashues and their friends for a meal at a St. John's steak restaurant. Tables were pushed together, and I noticed restaurant staff had placed a bottle of red wine on each table. The conversation was lively, the mood celebratory. There was no need to open the wine. It sat throughout the meal, uncorked, a mute testimony to the achievements this family has to celebrate.

What Addicts Have in Common

DARREN WRIGHTMAN HAD A GLOW ON. BUT IT WASN'T the glow that alcohol and drugs used to give him. Wrightman is from Walpole Island, a First Nations reserve not far from Windsor. His Aboriginal ancestry, bright blue sweater and stylishly cut long hair made him stand out from the rest of the sleepy crowd filling the auditorium. There were a lot of hard faces and hard bodies in the group. They were mostly non-Aboriginal men with tattoos and heavily muscled arms. A slow grin spread across Wrightman's face as the motivational speaker up front worked hard to stimulate the crowd. It was 7:30 on a Monday morning at the Brentwood Recovery Home.

"Come on, how many of you out there can say you've done anything for someone else this weekend?" shouted the speaker. "Or did you just lay around feeling sorry for yourselves, trying to get someone to do something for you?"

A slight man in front, wearing a grey V-necked sweater, raised his hand. "I helped my sister move this weekend," he said.

"How did that make you feel?" the speaker asked, but in a sneering kind of way.

"I felt good," said the man.

"You felt good!" the speaker repeated. "Well, what do you know about that? It feels good to help other people. Who'd have thought so? Not many of you, I'd say. Drinking and drugs used to feel good, didn't they? Now you've got to find other ways to feel good. And helping people is a great way to do that."

The facilitator continued his tirade against selfishness until the crowd broke for coffee and then into smaller discussion groups.

"You can tell how long a person has been here by the look on his or her face," said Charlie Baird, an addictions counsellor from Newfoundland raised at the Mount Cashel orphanage who came to Brentwood for help a decade ago and has been working there since. "We take a before and after picture, and many people hardly recognize themselves when their three months are up."

Darren Wrightman reflected on his own three months. "I feel great compared to where I was the day I walked in," he said. "I was broken, I was down. I didn't care if I was dead or alive. I didn't want to be around people, really. I could have sat in jail and been quite fine there."

Wrightman had been jailed for spousal assault, and the Brentwood Recovery Home was one of the few places that would take him with an outstanding criminal charge. "It wasn't my first choice," he told me. "A ninety-day program to quit drinking seemed like another jail sentence. But today I've changed. I feel better about myself. I've been able to dump a lot of the resentments and the pain that was kind of keeping me from wanting to live and keeping me in a bad place."

Health Canada funds fifty-six treatment centres as part

of its National Native Alcohol and Drug Abuse Program, and most Aboriginal addicts prefer treatment centres that are run by their own people. At the Brentwood Recovery Home there's no burning of sage and no sweat lodge. It's a bare-bones kind of place that operates on the belief addicts are the same, no matter what culture they come from.

Dr. Wilfred Gallant, a social work professor at the University of Windsor and a former addict, has written a book about Brentwood called *Sharing the Love That Frees Us*. Gallant's own positive experience at Brentwood led him to study what makes the centre's program work. From Father Charbonneau, he writes, he learned that an addict has replaced "the need for love, caring and sharing, intimacy, work, play, family, relations and so on" with "a misplaced obsession for lust, inordinate power, control, sexual prowess, workaholism, seduction, family dysfunction and pseudo relationships." According to the Brentwood definition of addiction, the substance or activity itself, whether it is alcohol, drugs or gambling, does not create the addict. An addict is created from some trauma early in life that leaves an emotional or spiritual void. "Each alcoholic is hurt, wounded or seriously offended at an early age, and carries this resentment, turmoil and confusion into later years, adopting a dysfunctional approach to life, people, situations and events," Gallant writes.

Darren Wrightman began drinking at the age of eight while living in a group home. "For me, alcoholism was about trying to change everybody," he said. "When it didn't work, it brought me down to my knees and into a whole lot of pain. I've learned to accept that the only thing I can change is myself, instead of always trying to change everything around me."

Karl S., twenty-two years old at the time, is also from Walpole Island. He allowed me to record one of his group sessions.

This was his seventh week at Brentwood. He leaned forward so that the men seated in the small circle could hear him better. He had been asked to talk about "conformity."

"I didn't give a fuck about a lot of things," Karl told the group. "Like, I was supposed to spend time with my girlfriend, I wouldn't do that. I'd be out screwing around with some other chick. I never conformed to anything. I didn't give a shit about nothing, especially the law. I never conformed to being a big brother, a good son. School, I was terrible in school. I didn't want to listen, I guess, I don't know. That's my understanding, anyways, of conforming. I just didn't give a fuck, plain and simple."

"Life was yours, eh?" said the alumni member who was facilitating this discussion.

"Yeah, life was mine, and I lived it how I wanted to live it," Karl said. "I didn't care how people thought about me. I'd go into a party where I had six or seven enemies and I wouldn't give a shit; I'd walk into that party by myself. If I wasn't allowed somewhere, I'd still go."

"So what does conforming mean to you now, as we're sitting here?"

"I'm starting to listen, not going and doing those stupid things that I used to do," Karl said. "Abide by the law, try to listen more, I guess. I'm just thinking about life now, like ahead, what am I going to do? I never thought about what I was going to do. I was always going to grow up and be a gangster. My plan then was to sell drugs and knock people's heads off and rob for what I need."

"Alcoholism in many definitions is a disease of self," Brentwood's executive director, Don Russell, explained during an interview in his small office. "AA will use terms like 'self-will run riot'. It's self, self, self, me, me, me and I, I, I. So any opportunity we have, we make sure they get the message that there's a 'we'. There are others. There's family. There's friends. There's peers you work with, and so on. It's the 'we' that's going to get us out of addiction."

Russell has a Master's degree in social work and a lot of addiction counselling experience. But it's his experience as a recovered addict that seems most valuable to people at Brentwood. A few years ago he took over the reins from the centre's founder, Father Paul Charbonneau. Russell had big shoes to fill, because for many years the centre was animated by Charbonneau's charismatic zeal to reform addicts. From the outset, Charbonneau tried to create a family atmosphere.

"I felt the minute I walked in here there was something special about this place," Darren Wrightman told me. "I felt like I was meant to be here for a long, long time. There is a lot of struggle involved in recovery, because we've got to look at ourselves. There is a lot of pain, a lot of hurt, but it's totally worth it. Now I want to live, and I want to help people again. I was a good person at one time. Then a bad person, then a good person, then a bad person. Now I'm back to trying to be on the upswing."

Karl S. was also looking ahead. "I want to be a drug and alcohol addiction counsellor in Walpole and help the young guys," he told me over lunch. "I got young guys smoking rock [cocaine]. I was contributing evil on my res. I realize that drugs, it's a really big epidemic on Walpole right now. So it makes me feel bad because I contributed a lot to it. Now I feel like I should go back to Walpole and try to help out, try to change people's lives, because I got a big influence on Walpole. There's a lot of kids who look up to me."

"When the alcoholic makes this breakthrough," Father Charbonneau told me, "he begins to experience a peace and a freedom, a joy. They experience what a human being really is and what it means to live as a person, and experience all the joys and the strengths of being truly human and allowing others to be human with you."

"When you start hearing them talk about their children, when it's not about 'me' so much anymore, they're on their way," Don Russell added. "That's what I look for. When *they* bring up the children, instead of me, they're really on their way then. That's good."

Staying sober wasn't easy for Wrightman or Karl S. once they left Brentwood. In the months following his first stay, Wrightman relapsed and tried desperately to be readmitted. The centre is used to this, but it walks a fine balance between providing help and creating dependency. Clients are encouraged to become independent and seek resources outside Brentwood to remain sober. Wrightman did return for a time, and then moved to Sarnia, where he worked at a call centre. Today he's sober, back home and working on the reserve.

Karl S. was back on the street for eleven months before he got additional help from the CanAm Indian Friendship Centre in Windsor. He'd been sober ten months when I spoke to him in November 2007. He will soon become a father, is working and plans to go to university in the fall of 2008 for training that will make him an addiction therapist. Karl believes Brentwood got him started on the right road, but says it was returning to his people's traditions and ceremonies that helped him the most.

7

The Miracle at Alkali Lake

THE COMMUNITY OF ALKALI LAKE, BRITISH COLUMBIA, became famous in the 1980s. The media was all over the story of how this First Nations reserve had successfully lowered its high rate of alcoholism. Since then there have been countless other stories and reports on Alkali Lake, including a moving documentary entitled *The Honour of All*. A U.S. Aboriginal filmmaker named Phil Lucas, with the assistance of Phil Lane Jr. at Four Worlds International Institute, used the actual people involved in Alkali Lake's recovery movement as actors in the film. They recreate the drama of their own lives, adding a strong air of authenticity to the storytelling. The stars of the film are Phyllis and Andy Chelsea.

I called the Chelseas a little apprehensively, thinking they'd be sick of the media attention they'd already received, and I was pleasantly surprised when Phyllis suggested I come to the reserve for the AA Round Up and Camp Out in July 2006. It's an annual event, and I learned that similar camp outs are held by AA throughout North America during the summer. When Phyllis faxed me the itinerary, she told me to expect things to be a bit "rough." I said that was fine. It was a camp out, after all, and I expected to sleep in a tent. What I hadn't expected was to find the Chelseas living in such rough conditions all year round.

I travelled by bus to Williams Lake, the closest centre to Alkali Lake. Phyllis Chelsea offered to pick me up at the bus stop since the reserve, also called Esk'et, is some distance from town. It was a long bus ride, about six hours from Vancouver, but I enjoyed every minute of it. The scenery through the Fraser Canyon was stunning, with lots of sagebrush along the way. Tshaukuesh's son, Matshen Penashue, had asked me to bring back some sweetgrass and sage from my trip. In the lives of newly sober Aboriginals in Canada, Alkali Lake and the Chelseas (Matshen also wanted both their autographs) symbolize something very important, a spiritual force.

Phyllis arrived at the bus depot in a truck driven by her daughter Ivy. At sixty-three, Phyllis is a small, lively woman with large glasses. She quickly put me at ease with her warmth and good humour. It became clear right away, too, that she and her daughter are very close. Ivy was seven when her mother stopped drinking. Strong-willed and determined, she was the reason Phyllis sobered up. In 1972 Ivy told her mother she preferred living with her sober grandmother and wasn't going back home. The threat gave Phyllis enough motivation to stop drinking immediately. It took a while for Andy to follow suit, but he did. For a year or two, they were the only sober adults their age in the community. With courage and patience, they began working hard to change that. As chief, Andy banished the truck driver that brought alcohol from Williams

Lake during "cheque time" out of town, along with a drunken priest and his lover, the community's only nurse. When Phyllis became welfare officer in the community, she gave out food vouchers instead of money. For Phyllis to get the job in the first place, the Chelseas had to seize the position from the indian agent. "I knocked his glasses off," Andy recounted to me later, "when he told Phyllis she was too stupid to administer welfare on the reserve." When the community's non-Aboriginal shopkeeper refused to cooperate with the food voucher system, Phyllis started her own small store. The Chelseas also confronted drinkers by showing up at party houses and asking why people weren't looking after their children. One by one, friends and family members stopped drinking, until the number of alcoholics in the community shrank to a minority.

The strong sobriety ethic that was created exists to this day, though dealing with alcoholism and other social problems in the community, such as sexual abuse, has not lifted Alkali Lake out of poverty. Nor has it kept all the Chelsea children sober. One son recently returned from an alcoholism treatment centre. The Chelseas look back on their accomplishment documented in *The Honour of All* with pride as they head into retirement, but not with comfort. They are living what Andy wryly calls the "Indian dream"—they're broke. Their predicament is a case study of the systemic barriers Aboriginal people face in achieving a standard of living equal to that of other Canadians.

On the way to Alkali Lake, we stopped to visit some friends of Phyllis and Ivy who operate a creative business on the Sugar Cane (T'exelc) reserve. Kristy Palmantier and Ted Moses make beautiful coffins with customized decorations. Phyllis joked that she wants a picture of Elvis painted on the inside lid of her coffin. "Close enough to kiss," Ivy said with a laugh. The decorations depicted hopeful images of hummingbirds and eagles, bright flowers and inspirational words to see the departed off with respect and dignity. Kristy and Ted served us a lovely meal of deer meat and vegetables. Woven into the conversation were disturbing stories of police harassment and horrible car accidents that have occurred on the unsafe roads linking the reserves around Williams Lake. The family's teenage son did the dishes after supper, and the comings and goings of relatives and friends during the evening made it clear that strong family and community ties exist despite the marginalization and economic hardship that characterize so many First Nations reserves.

Alkali Lake is a tidy, picturesque reserve of 400 people set in a valley in the B.C. Interior. The Shuswap people's traditional territory is real cowboy country.

"My father was a hill-rider," Andy Chelsea explained when I met him at the Chelseas' home. "He'd ride his horse down the steepest hills, whooping it up, wowing the spectators." Andy brought out pictures of his father and newspaper clippings about rodeos held in the 1950s. There's still an annual rodeo on the reserve each summer.

"If you came around here in July in the forties and fifties, you'd only find five or six elders on the reserve," he said. "Everybody else was out in the meadows, making hay for their cattle and horses and putting in gardens." As the reserve population grew, the land available for these activities shrank.

The reserves allotted to B.C. First Nations are much smaller than the reserves in the rest of the country. Andy and Phyllis got tired of waiting for the government to recognize their people's territory with a land claim agreement or treaty, so they moved off reserve to the edge of a nearby ranch, where they fenced off a small acreage of their own to keep a few horses.

Canada has the sixth highest standard of living in the world, according to the United Nations Human Development Index. Using the U.N. formula, which measures life expectancy, literacy levels, rates of education and child welfare, First Nations in Canada rank beside Brazil for sixty-ninth place. The disparity in life expectancy is particularly stark. Canadian men live 75.7 years on average, women 81.4 years. For Aboriginal people, the average life expectancy for males is sixty-two years; for females, it's sixty-nine. I didn't have to look much further than the Chelseas' home to understand why there's such poor health on many reserves.

Like the other houses at Alkali Lake, the Chelseas' home was constructed by Canada's Central Mortgage and Housing Corporation, and it is so riddled with toxic mould it has been condemned. CMHC housing on reserves is so mould-infested, in fact—Statistics Canada reports it in 50 per cent of First Nations homes—that it has become a nasty joke. The houses were built using loans advanced to First Nations bands, and those loans are paid off over time by charging residents rent.

"People think we get free housing on reserves," Phyllis pointed out. "We don't. We bought our house here. Our children rent theirs from the band council. And all the houses are mouldy."

The Chelseas have done their best to paint and wallpaper over the mould in their home. Phyllis had even hung a cotton sheet on one wall to hide the blue cheese-like growth underneath. She has a constant cough that she believes is associated with the mould. Nonetheless, wood heat makes the kitchen and living room cosy, as do the shelves of mementos marking the couple's many accomplishments. Alongside pictures of their five children and ten grandchildren I noticed framed certificates from various organizations recognizing the Chelseas' work to encourage sobriety, Phyllis' honorary degree from the University of British Columbia and her statuette from the Order of British Columbia. Although she had recently retired from teaching the Shuswap language, she hadn't been able to put away any money for her later years.

"We always needed the money for something else," she said. Phyllis had just been diagnosed with osteoporosis but couldn't follow the doctor's orders. "He says I should drink milk and juice, but I can't afford to," she told me. The Chelseas' oldest son died from diabetes complications a few years after *The Honour of All* was made. Their daughter and three other sons live on the reserve. The family pools its money, and during my visit they were trying to raise $60 so that their youngest son, who has five children, could get his electricity restored. It had been shut off when he couldn't pay the bill.

Andy Chelsea is a broad-shouldered man who, at six feet tall, towers over his tiny wife. Like Ivy, he is strong-willed and opinionated, with a dry sense of humour. But he hadn't worked for three years, he told me; the band had been running a deficit, so Chelsea quit his job with the council to save the cost of a salary. He thought he'd get rehired when the project grant he'd applied for came through, but instead the band hired a younger person to do the work. Andy served as Alkali Lake's chief on and off for decades, always running a fiscally sound administration. During the previous election, he had run again for the chief's job, that time unsuccessfully. So Andy and Phyllis found themselves on welfare, receiving just $307 a month. Despite the province's great wealth, in 2003

B.C. had the largest number of people living in poverty in Canada—20.1 per cent of the population, compared with 11 per cent in Prince Edward Island. It hasn't improved much since.

"When we get really hungry, a deer'll come down over that hill there," said Andy with a grin, pointing out the kitchen window, "and let us shoot him for food. We won't starve as long as there are enough deer."

Phyllis and Andy still got phone calls and e-mails from recovering addicts looking for their support, they told me. They were trying to maintain their phone and internet service as long as they could, but worried the cost might become prohibitive. Ideally, they'd like to have a 1-800 number to keep up the volunteer work they're doing. The Chelseas' financial situation will improve when Andy turns sixty-five, and he and Phyllis both receive compensation for the abuse they suffered at St. Joseph's residential school.

Phyllis and Ivy agreed to take me to the site of the former school, which was run by the Roman Catholic Oblates. Phyllis went there between the ages of seven and sixteen. Her memories were very traumatic, she warned me. We drove there together in Ivy's truck. Most of the original buildings have been torn down, and the large property that once contained the school, dormitories and housing for nuns and priests is now a ranch. Loud angry dogs patrolled the property, preventing us from leaving our vehicle. There was enough left of the former facility to send a shiver through Phyllis, though; she said she considers it an evil place.

Boys at the school had to dig the irrigation ditch still surrounding the property, Phyllis told me. She remembered seeing Andy out there with his shovel. The girls did domestic work. The 300 Shuswap children at the school produced food on the makeshift farm, but there was never enough to go around. The children believed dead babies were buried in the powerhouse, which is still standing, though that horror story is not among the atrocities committed at St. Joseph's that the Law Commission of Canada documented in a report on institutional child abuse in Canada called "Restoring Dignity."

"Parents who withheld their children from the school were subject to fines or imprisonment," the Law Commission report says. "When parents requested that their children spend one month with them in the summer, both the Oblate Mission and the Department of Indian Affairs refused this request." Andy Chelsea was at St. Joseph's for seven years. He ran away at sixteen, when he knew his parents wouldn't be prosecuted for not taking him back to the school.

Phyllis still remembers the terror of her first day at school. She and other children were loaded into a cattle car and driven there, holding onto a steel bar to keep from falling off.

"I can still feel the breeze blowing up through my skirt," she told me. "I cried and cried, and so did my mother."

One hundred former Shuswap students say they were sexually abused at the school, and two priests have been convicted so far. Some children tried to poison themselves to escape the school's severe corporal punishment. Andy Chelsea wasn't the first to run away. In 1902 a boy of eight named Duncan Sticks, from Alkali Lake, was found dead after he escaped. No one from the school had bothered to look for him, and his parents weren't told he was missing. The Shuswap people tried then to persuade authorities to close the school, without success. It remained open until 1981. The Law Commission report states that the school severely damaged Shuswap society, leading to "the loss of parenting skills, breakdown of families, loss of pride in their culture and heritage, suicide and physical problems."

Somehow, despite everything they'd been through as children, Andy and Phyllis Chelsea had the strength to lead their community out of the dark hole it had fallen into. When we spoke Phyllis seemed more at peace with the past than did Andy.

"Living on the reserve is the same as residential school. Nothing's changed. It's still controlled, but now chief and council are the priests and nuns," he said. "The principal of the whole thing is the Department of Indian Affairs. When you think about it, it's the same. You're still not allowed to go develop any land. You're not allowed to go against the principal's policies."

The local real estate listings helped to explain why the Shuswap are so economically marginalized today. The Springfield Ranch, for example, was selling for $3.35 million. The listing said the ranch has 2,441 acres of land. Traditionally Shuswap territory, the property was given by the British Crown in 1862 to five gold miners, new arrivals to British Columbia, who were awarded the land simply because they "occupied" it. A law called the "right of occupation" applied at that time. The land tract was kept in one family for a few generations, then sold and resold, reaping profits for individuals along the way. Andy Chelsea wondered aloud why none of his people ever got land by right of occupation, even after thousands of years of living there. Instead, the Aboriginal people of British Columbia were moved onto postage-stamp–sized reserves.

After a lifetime of watching white ranchers and logging companies get rich from former Shuswap pasture land, Andy Chelsea did something about it in 1991, when he fenced off the acre or so of land eight miles from the reserve for his family's house and pasture. A neighbouring rancher claimed the acreage belonged to him, and there were threats of eviction.

Andy thinks his stature in the community protected him when authorities tried to carry that eviction out.

"I got my youngest son, Kevin, to stand up in the back of the truck with a video camera," he explained.

"We couldn't find a tape to put in it," Phyllis added, a gleam in her eye.

"When they saw Kevin aiming the video camera at them, the RCMP left, then the forestry people left, then the Indian Affairs guy, until finally there was just me and the rancher," Andy continued. "I didn't say much and he left, too."

In the years that followed, Andy paid off the mortgage on his house. Although the house has been condemned, he'd rather stay on the land he's fenced than take something that might come up on the reserve. He doesn't have legal title to it, though. He'd hoped to start a small logging business, but he couldn't get a loan.

"The funding is not going to come from chief and council, it's not going to come from the Department of Indian Affairs, it's not going to come from a bank, so what chance have you got?" he said.

I stayed at the Chelseas' home while I was on the reserve, but we ate all our meals at the AA camp out. It was as much from necessity as for fun. A logging truck carrying a load of timber had knocked out the Chelseas' power. Andy was livid, because the band council had given the logging contract to a non-Aboriginal contractor. Fortunately there was lots of food available to barbeque at the camp out, where a festive mood prevailed. There were games of horseshoes, rides in a rodeo-style horse and carriage, music and dancing.

The cheerful and loving support I saw the Chelseas offer each other was inspiring. They didn't expect anyone to rescue them from their predicament. They were just hoping their children would have a better life.

"My granddaughter wants to live in Paris," Phyllis said. "I told her I hope her dream comes true. But I tell all my children they've got to come back here in the summer and make the hay like we always did. Even after Andy and I are gone. I want to be up there in heaven, looking down at them making the hay."

A sense of humour is obviously one of the things that has kept this family going. Following my visit, one of the Chelseas' grandchildren sent me an e-mail that details how you can tell when you're on the "rez":

You mix Carnation milk and water for your cereal.

You use a rag for a gas cap.

You owe money to at least three people.

When somebody falls down, you laugh and then ask if they are okay.

You use dishwashing liquid for bubble bath or laundry soap.

You've gotten chased by or run from the police on foot and got away.

You have reusable bacon grease in a container on your stove.

Your only income is from powwow singing, powwow dancing or fixing cars.

You've driven for two weeks on a flat tire that you just keep filling with air.

You've left a social gathering with a plate full of food.

You use jelly and jam jars as your cups.

You use Vaseline to shine your shoes.

Your curtain is a sheet.

You've drunk alcohol by the age of thirteen or younger.

You've smoked before the age of nine.

You learned to drive at the age of twelve.

Your aunts or uncles come to visit and never leave.

8

Healing in Hollow Water

IN 1992, WHILE I WAS ON THE BOARD OF THE WRITERS
Alliance of Newfoundland and Labrador, there was an opportunity to take a few writers from St. John's to Sheshatshiu.
Author Roberta Buchanan agreed to run some workshops on
journal writing with me, and Dereck O'Brien came along to
talk about his book, *Suffer Little Children*, about the years he
was abused in foster care at the Mount Cashel Orphanage.

O'Brien's presence in the community created a buzz; some
Innu leaders were concerned about raising the issue of sexual
abuse without having therapeutic services available. There was
even talk of cancelling the reading, but under pressure from
the Innu public it went ahead, and hundreds of people packed
into the hall to hear Dereck read. Afterwards, there was an
avalanche of requests from individuals who wanted to tell
O'Brien their own stories of abuse. Dereck generously agreed
to speak to as many people as he could, going with them in
private to hear their stories. The journal writing workshop
prompted an outpouring of grief from those in attendance like

nothing Roberta or I had ever witnessed; so many people were in tears that we were unable to continue. Even at the airport, people who'd come to see us off passed Dereck slips of paper. He would acknowledge each one, then put it into his pocket. "People need to tell someone," he explained to us later, "so they tell me." He said it happened not only in Aboriginal communities but in many of the Newfoundland communities he visited. Eventually, O'Brien simply stopped touring with the book. But this glimpse of the extent of abuse suffered by people in Sheshatshiu was something I never forgot, and it was brought vividly back to mind when I visited the Ojibway community of Hollow Water.

This First Nations reserve, also known as Wanipigow by its residents, is located 150 kilometres north of Winnipeg. The community's name refers to a whirlpool near the reserve that is created by the force of water spilling into Lake Winnipeg from a nearby river, creating a depression or hollow. The whirlpool is chaotic, its energy created by spinning whorls of water. Circles of turbulence.

Circles are sacred shapes for the Anishnawbe people (also known as Ojibway), and in Hollow Water circles of people have been coming together for twenty years to heal the turbulence of sexual abuse that once threatened to engulf the community. A sophisticated therapeutic process called Community Holistic Circle Healing (CHCH) was invented here, and it is considered one of the best ways stop the cycle of this most heinous crime. The people who developed this brave and innovative process believe it can rebuild Aboriginal societies, and they can't understand why Canadian policy makers have been so reluctant to support it.

Sexual abuse is considered a major cause of suicide and substance abuse in Aboriginal communities today. As part of a 1997 report for Corrections Canada called "The Four Circles of Hollow Water," Christine Sivell-Ferri visited Hollow Water and studied how the methodology used there tied in with Anishnawbe (Ojibway) ceremony and values. She writes: "The prevalent sexual traumatization of children in Hollow Water is not socially isolated. It is a manifestation of the dysfunction within Aboriginal communities across the continent. Dysfunction, including the sexual abuse of children, is a foreseeable outcome that has resulted from the deliberate intent of the dominant society to sever a people from themselves."

Twenty-three years ago, sexual abuse had become a way of life in Hollow Water. The social history of this community is the social history of many First Nations, Inuit and Metis communities, and it is only because courageous women like Burma Bushie are willing to talk about it, and to devote their lives to finding solutions, that we can ever hope to end it.

I met Burma Bushie for dinner one evening at the Healing Our Spirit conference, in Edmonton, after a presentation she'd made. Bushie is fifty-nine years old, with the confident bearing of a woman who has accomplished much in her lifetime. She is by nature soft-spoken and retiring, and I could feel the effort she was making to once again tell a stranger her difficult story, though it's a story she frequently shares in public to inspire others.

"If you had seen my community back in the seventies when there was so much chaos, visible chaos, you would have written us off," she began.

People stumbled around drunk in public, Bushie said. Women were bruised and beaten. Children cowered. She described the chaos in greater detail in the 1997 Corrections Canada study. "Alcohol abuse [was] at its highest point [then]," the report quotes her as saying. "You could find a party in the community any time of the day or any day of the week. There was violence between men. There were gangs back then. There was also violence against women, both physically, sexually, mentally and psychologically. But the physical violence and sexual assaults were the most visible." Bushie told me that women did not start drinking until the sixties. "That's when our community started to go downhill," she said. "Prior to that the women were holding everything together."

Bushie herself was sexually abused by her grandfather between the ages of six and nine. She was raped by someone else when she was just twelve.

"It got to the point where I would eat and eat and eat and never know that I was full. Or I would go for days without eating and not know I was hungry. I was totally disconnected from my body," she has said of the damage the abuse caused.

When children are assaulted, Bushie believes, they lose their spirit. "I have been looking at my community for a long time," she told me. "The weakest piece in the community is the spiritual. We started to use all these drugs and alcohol, pills and what-not to numb the pain. That separated us from our spirit even more. Your spirit's home is your body, so if you are putting all this bad stuff in your body, does your spirit want to live there?"

Sexual abuse is not solely an Aboriginal problem, of course. According to Dr. William Marshall of Queen's University and Y.M. Fernandez of Ontario's Bath Institute, a Canadian woman is sexually abused every seven minutes. One in every four girls and one in every eight boys are sexually molested in childhood. The specialists describe sexual abusers as insecure manipulators who pretend to be paragons of virtue to disguise their behaviour or to build up their own egos.

"Research has found that sexual offenders lack self-confidence. Many child molesters, in particular, are unassertive and somewhat passive, easily led and readily taken advantage of by others," Marshall and Fernandez write in the 1997 policy paper for Corrections Canada. "This...makes them feel resentful and somehow entitled to make themselves feel better at the expense of others."

Alcoholics and other addicts are more likely to be sexual abusers, they say. "Once sexual abuse commences, feelings of guilt or fear will facilitate further alcohol or drug use and this may escalate into addiction. Prolonged addictions wear away social restraints so that sexual offending may occur as part of a more general breakdown in appropriate behaviour."

Appropriate behaviour had so degenerated in Hollow Water by the early 1980s that Burma Bushie and a handful of other women had to meet in secret to talk about it. The women estimated that three of every four persons on the reserve had been sexually abused at some point during their lives, and that one of every three persons was an abuser. They knew it had to be stopped. But how?

What happened next is in the realm of miracles. Bushie and a small group of men and women, about twenty-four of them by 1986, looked straight into the heart of darkness in their community and turned the power of evil into a power of such goodness that Judge Murray Sinclair of the Manitoba Provincial Court allowed them to deal with sex offenders on their own terms, rather than hand them over to the courts. Community Holistic Circle Healing doesn't send sex offenders to jail for one simple reason: jail doesn't change their behaviour.

"The easy thing to do is just to deny everything and go sit in jail for a couple of months, because in many cases in Manitoba we're finding that the sentences for incarceration are two years less a day," Bushie told me. "I believe you have to serve a third of that sentence. So on good behaviour you can be out in a few months. That's the easy way out."

By contrast, the CHCH process sets in motion a community-wide response to a disclosure of sexual abuse. First a trained team meets with the victim and ensures that he or she is safe. If it's an incest situation, the child is taken out of the home. If not, the child is kept in a secure setting where medical help and counselling are provided. Another team immediately confronts the abuser, whatever the time of day or night. They do their best to get the abuser to admit to the crime. If he or she does not, the police are called in. If the abuser admits guilt to the team, criminal charges are still laid, but those charges are stayed until the CHCH process is completed. It takes five years.

"We bring that person into a circle," Bushie explained during our interview. "We ask them to tell us what they've done. In a lot of cases when we start working they can't tell all the details. With each circle they add on and add on as they begin to feel the support. They begin to understand that they are not being judged, that we're here to help them, that we want the crimes to stop and we want them to become productive, balanced people. They have to have weekly sessions with their abuse worker. They have to have weekly sessions with the therapist and counsellor. They have to have weekly sessions with the human sexuality program. We, as a team, sit with them on a monthly basis."

The second circle starts four months later, and in it the offender is asked to sit with both CHCH workers and the offender's nuclear family. The offender must tell his partner and children what he's done. It is very hard, Bushie acknowledged, to face your immediate family and admit sexual abuse. Even harder is the third circle, where the offender must face his extended family and do the same thing. Then there's a fourth circle.

"This is where they tell the whole community," Bushie explained. "If a person can go through those four circles, then we're convinced that he or she is committed to healing and will do everything to continue. If that person is not able to complete the circles, then we will honour the courts."

A judge is invited to attend the fourth circle to pass sentence, a sentence that is usually determined on the recommendation of the community. Then there's a feast to celebrate reconciliation between the offender and the victim and among the wider circle of family and friends.

"I don't believe for one minute that people are using us," Bushie emphasized. "They find out very quickly how difficult it is to face their own people."

A lot is accomplished with each telling of a sexual abuse story in these circles. The public learns first-hand how harmful the activity is for victims. Transparency ensures that abusers are held to account for their actions for as long as they remain in the community. Therapy heals the offenders (few sexual offenders who've been through the CHCH program reoffend) and the victim.

It's an exhausting process for the small CHCH team, though. In 1997, seven workers paid 352 home visits, according to that year's report for the Solicitor General. The circles involve so many people it can sometimes take ten to twelve hours to complete them. One disclosure may bring out a history of sexual abuse that involves many members of an extended family. In 1997 alone, 282 circles were held. The pay for CHCH workers is not high for the number of hours they devote to their jobs, but they keep at it because the benefits for the entire community are so tangible. As the rate of sexual abuse declined, so did the rates of addiction.

Ike Fehr owns a small hotel in the neighbouring Metis community of Manigotogan. I stayed there while doing my research. His hotel is the nearest place to Hollow Water to buy alcohol or play video lottery terminals (VLTs). Fehr estimates that over the twenty years he's had the hotel, his business has dropped by more than 60 per cent. Burma Bushie estimates 80 per cent of the community's adults now abstain from alcohol. Whatever the number, Fehr told me alcohol sales have dropped so substantially he's planning to sell the business.

According to Bushie, the CHCH process has transformed not just Hollow Water but the three neighbouring Metis communities as well, a combined population of 1,000 people. "At first we were saying alcoholism was the problem; suicide was the problem; child neglect was the problem; kids dropping out of school was the problem," she told me. "The more we learned about ourselves, the more we learned about our community. Then we started touching on sexual abuse. There were sixty people at one workshop: church workers, single moms and the general membership. We couldn't ignore the problem, because we were faced with actual numbers. The stats were very shocking. It was a crisis. People disclosed because of all the work we had been doing and because people had sobered up. A lot of us have gone down that road of abusing alcohol to numb the pain. Thoughts of suicide were never far away from our minds, so we had travelled that road, and we knew what the symptoms were. Those were awesome times that sent us deeper."

Burma Bushie is a deeply spiritual person, as are her colleagues in the CHCH process. They have to be spiritual to do the work they do. Every year, an American woman who works with prisoners on death row visits Hollow Water for solace.

"She told us she needs to come to a place where people are actually willing to forgive and willing to work with people who offend," Bushie told me. "I think about her often when we are struggling. I think of what she has to face."

There's more balance in the lives of Hollow Water's people today. They've come out of the darkness, Bushie said. "There is definitely a reason why my community was chosen to deal with this problem. We really believe that we are instruments of the Creator, of our grandfathers and grandmothers. It's time to heal from all this. I really feel privileged that my community has taken on the task to show others. I think my community offers hope to other communities."

Many other rivers flow into Lake Winnipeg, and there's a First Nations reserve on almost all of them. Sexual abuse remains a serious problem for these places. Many of the children from nearby reserves are brought to Hollow Water for foster care. The small community of 400 is in danger of being overwhelmed by the needs of its neighbours.

In 2007, the CHCH received $100,000 each from the justice departments of Canada and Manitoba. The program has been proven to work, and it's a lot cheaper than putting people in jail. Some other funding has been provided by the Aboriginal Healing Foundation for a wilderness program that is bringing back the use of sled dogs. This money pays salaries, but that's about all. The CHCH team operates out of a split-level house where quarters are cramped. There's a large room set up with sewing machines and a table for scrapbooking projects and quilting, some of the therapeutic activities that are used with offenders. Bernadette Hardisty and Donna Smith are two of the counsellors I met. They told me they used to hold circles in the basement of the CHCH house, but frequent flooding has made the space unusable.

"If we're working with family members there's hardly any room to breathe in this little space," Hardisty said, referring to their office. "That's one of the challenges. We don't have enough space."

"People from all over the country phone," Smith added, "and they ask if they can come here and work on issues. We have to turn them away, because we don't have a place for them. A lot of people assume that we have a facility, a treatment place, but we don't."

Burma Bushie dreams of a wilderness healing lodge where families from other communities can be housed while they go through the process. CHCH has developed a training program to teach members of other Aboriginal communities how to do the work, but funding is always too tight to export it. I asked Bushie what she'd like Canadians to understand about the work her community has been doing.

"I think the Canadian public needs to understand the long-term impacts of colonization," she told me. "They need to understand the practices used by government and by churches to totally wipe out the Aboriginal nations. There has to be a recognition that this happened. There has to be acknowledgement. We've come a long way, and our struggle should be celebrated, not ridiculed. That kind of acceptance and acknowledgement would go a long way to make the struggle less painful. This is our fight, and we will do it. We are up for the challenge, and we will do it."

As Burma Bushie told me, "I say to government officials and Canadians that you can either be on the side of helping us or you can decide to make the struggle that much harder. I would like to believe there are good people out there regardless of what positions they hold in government, and I believe that goodness is going to triumph."

Marcel Hardisty, a fisherman I met at Hollow Water, is also the community's administrator of social development programs. He and his wife, Bernadette, are raising a young boy from a nearby reserve whose parents committed suicide. He met me one morning at the band council office; Hardisty showed me a chart that community members had drawn up as a blueprint for their future. Government bureaucracies are lousy at helping to solve human problems, he said.

"Bureaucracies, institutions, government programs—all have a need to maintain and justify their own existence, so peoples' needs become secondary," Hardisty told me. "These institutions were founded to meet people's needs, but for the sake of maintaining existence, people's needs become secondary."

"What do you think is needed to help communities where there is still so much suffering?" I asked him.

"I think people need to be supported in their home communities, in their home environment," he replied. "They should be able to develop what they have, what has always sustained people in that region, whether it's harvesting berries, fish, wildlife, timber, minerals. People should have a say in what goes on in their backyards in terms of the resources of the land, and people will need help to get the skills they need to mobilize and develop their ideas. When I was working as welfare officer for Hollow Water, I asked the Indian Affairs department to fast-track some of the dollars they were going to spend towards welfare on an economic development fund, so we could develop training programs, develop people's self-esteem, educate them. Back in the seventies, that would have been around $8 to $10 million. We could have created an economic base for the people. Well, the powers, the bureaucracy, the Indian Affairs department wouldn't see that or couldn't see that. It certainly would have been money well spent. It would have created a people that would be self-sufficient once again."

Hollow Water, like Alkali Lake, is famous for the social revolution started by its residents. But its successful formula for social change has not spread outside its borders, nor has the community prospered. Unless the conditions that first plunged people into the spiral of addiction and abuse are removed, the beauty and symbolism of the Anishnawbe circle may become a metaphor instead for a vicious cycle of suffering. As Burma Bushie told me, more funding would help fast-track solutions for other reserves but nothing can stop the momentum at Hollow Water today. "I truly appreciate all the help that we've gotten from government up to now, and I would hope that help continues. That's all I ask for. The rest of the work that needs to be done is definitely on the part of Aboriginal people. We have to do the work. We have to rebuild our communities and we have to heal ourselves. All of that is our responsibility. I hope that the help continues to come our way."

The Trauma Connection

AT THE AGE OF FORTY-THREE, DR. CORNELIA WIEMAN IS Canada's youngest Aboriginal psychiatrist, and one of just a few in the profession today. Wieman is carrying on the work of Dr. Clare Brant, Canada's first Aboriginal psychiatrist, in raising awareness of the distinct mental health needs of the country's Indigenous inhabitants. She's also trying to bring more Aboriginals into the field by serving as a role model, but she's acutely aware of the many barriers preventing this. Principal among them is the mental health condition of the young people living on Canada's impoverished reserves and in Inuit and Metis communities. Many suffer from a condition known as "intergenerational trauma."

Nel Wieman escaped the worst effects of this kind of trauma because she was adopted. She was born at Little Grand Rapids, Manitoba, a First Nations reserve, but raised by a Dutch family in Thunder Bay after her birth mother died tragically. Wieman studied medicine and psychiatry at McMaster

University in Hamilton, Ontario, and after graduation practised at the mental health clinic on the nearby Six Nations reserve. There she was befriended by Roberta Jamieson, a well-known Mohawk lawyer who is now CEO of the National Aboriginal Achievement Foundation. Wieman's connection with the Jamieson family, and her other friendships on the reserve, helped her to reconnect with her Aboriginal heritage. Her time at Six Nations also strengthened her commitment to resolving the effects of intergenerational trauma. Today, besides teaching, Wieman conducts research for the University of Toronto's Indigenous Health Research Development program and the Faculty of Medicine.

"I think we're dealing with generations of people who have been damaged by colonialism," Wieman told me during a tour of the Six Nations reserve in her truck in January 2006. "The way that people have been treated by the dominant culture makes them feel dispirited, feel hopeless, feel devalued, and so people turn to things like addictions as a way of coping— self-medicating, not really wanting to be here, because their situation is just so intolerable."

The term "intergenerational trauma" was coined in the mid-1980s by a U.S. scholar, Maria Yellow Horse Brave Heart, to describe what happens when an ethnic group is traumatized over an extended period of time. "Forced assimilation and cumulative losses across generations involving language, culture and spirituality contribute to the breakdown of the family kinship networks and social structures," Dr. Brave Heart writes in *Healing and Mental Health for Native Americans: Speaking in Red*. "The historical legacy and the current psychosocial conditions contribute to ongoing intergenerational traumas."

Peter Mancall, author of the book *Deadly Medicine,* holds a view similar to that of sociologist Richard Thatcher in believing that the relationship between Aboriginal people and alcohol in North America began with the fur trade. There doesn't appear to have been an Aboriginal recipe before then even for home brew. "The Indians' demand for durable commodities such as guns and blankets declined over time as they acquired as many of them as they could reasonably use," Mancall writes. "Their demand for alcohol, by contrast, seemed to be constant. Since Indians could not or would not produce alcohol for themselves, and since no alcoholic drink lasts long, Indian drinkers had to return to traders to get more. Thus, alcohol became a highly valued object of trade."

Mancall combed archives in Canada and the United States for references to alcohol and North America's Indigenous inhabitants. He found many. In 1720, Mancall writes, an Iroquois man made the comment that traders brought so much rum it was "as if water out of a fountain." First Nations transgressors were forgiven by their own people if they were drunk when an offence was committed. According to Mancall, "The ability of attackers to escape punishment in this way suggests that communities accepted the idea that liquor was responsible for their actions; it made no sense to punish the person who committed the crime when the true offender was alcohol." Mancall also identifies the terrible conditions that made alcohol so appealing to eastern woodlands Indians and other Aboriginal people: "The death that daily surrounded and threatened them then is almost incomprehensible to us now. We know that the population of American Indians declined by at least 90 per cent by the end of the colonial period, mostly because of the spread of epidemic diseases. But it is difficult to grasp what it must have been like for Indians in a village when smallpox or measles swept through, killing half or more of the community, and then to have to migrate to a new area to create a new community, only to have the new village assaulted by more pathogens. Add to the recurring epidemics the periodic participation of many Indians in wars and the threats posed to communities by an expanding, land-hungry colonial population and it seems obvious that these Indians constantly battled tragedy and disaster. Death was everywhere, and it ripped families apart, upset the social order, interfered with vital economic pursuits, and eroded the social ties needed to hold communities together."

Despite the many catastrophes Aboriginal people experienced after the arrival of Europeans, Aboriginals in Canada persevered with amazing resiliency until the middle of the twentieth century, when they were forced off their remaining land bases to make way for hydroelectric projects, mines and logging operations. There was little community support available for people during this disruption, because everyone was affected in the same way. Social workers and welfare cheques sent in from the outside mostly made things worse, creating dependency and crushing self-esteem.

U.S. academic Dr. Sousan Abadian makes an important distinction between the trauma experienced by Aboriginal people and that of European Jews and the Japanese who survived the atomic bomb. "When Indigenous people were traumatized, they could not get healed by their ceremonies, because those had been outlawed," Abadian told me over dinner after presenting her theories at the Healing Our Spirit Worldwide conference in Edmonton. "The Japanese still had their ceremonies. There were still rabbis in other parts of the world to help the European Jews. Indigenous people lost everything, even their sacred lands."

In his office at the busy corner of Parliament and Queen streets in Toronto, Dr. Peter Menzies told me he sees the victims of this trauma daily. Menzies, who was born in 1953 on the Sagamok Anishnawbek First Nations reserve in northern Ontario, is the service manager for Aboriginal services at the Centre for Addiction and Mental Health and we spoke in January 2006. He believes the high addiction and suicide rates among his clients are symptoms of more than "two hundred years of government policies designed to eradicate and assimilate the Aboriginal peoples. Residential schools, the *Indian Act*, child welfare issues, the Indian agent and dispersing Aboriginal people onto reserves that leave few resources—it's all of that and more," he told me during an interview at the clinic.

The legacy of trauma he sees everyday troubles Menzies. "Intergenerational trauma is from individual to individual, family to family, community to community, nation to nation," he explained, also making a distinction between the trauma Aboriginals suffer and that associated with wartime experiences. "PTSD [post-traumatic stress disorder] looks at the individual; it doesn't look at the whole community, the families, the nation, the history, the whole apparatus of the state oppressing the people. Almost all Indigenous communities on earth are experiencing these phenomena."

Dr. Jane Simington is an Edmonton-based psychologist who has been counselling Aboriginal women in Canada's prisons for the past eighteen years. Simington believes the Canadian law passed in 1920 that forced Aboriginal parents to give up their children to residential schools is a major cause of today's social problems. The last residential school was closed in Saskatchewan in 1996.

"The trauma I see is huge, huge," Simington told me after her workshop at Healing Our Spirit Worldwide. "Children were ripped out of their homes at the age of five for residential schools, and they didn't come back until they were seventeen. Many of them had been abused physically and sexually. Their parents were, in the meantime, at home grieving their children, so they turned to alcohol. And the whole thing about parenting and loving is that they are learned behaviours. Residential school students didn't learn to parent. When the anxiety gets high they strike out, because they're angry at themselves, and so these little innocent ones are an easy target. Family violence is huge. When I was teaching parenting at the women's prison, they liked the videos I brought. Their words were, 'You show us how to do it, we've never seen it.' Almost all who come to my training have experienced significant family violence."

Alcoholism prevented Peter Menzies' parents from raising him. He was raised off the reserve like Nel Wieman, first by the Sisters of St. Joseph and later by the Children's Aid Society. Menzies is reminded every day of his own narrow escape from addiction by his Aboriginal clients, who make up the highest proportion of Toronto's homeless population. He would like to stop out-migration from reserves by making them better places for people to live.

"It's important to stop the brain drain," he told me, "and it's important to prevent more people from landing in homeless shelters and prisons. I've always maintained that alcohol and drugs are only symptoms. When I sit down with an Aboriginal person to provide counselling, I don't even deal with the drinking issues. I see guys who have left their community because they have so much trauma in them that they don't know how to deal with. The community can't deal with them, because they don't have the mental health services. Why is that? Why can't they stay in their communities or near their communities and get treatment for however long it takes to deal with this trauma that they're carrying?"

Menzies dreams one day of creating an addiction treatment centre that will help Aboriginal leaders who are still drinking to return to their reserves and better serve their people. "I watch some of our leaders, and I see a lot of pain and suffering. Why do their personalities look defeated? Why don't I see a head held high? As a therapist I think, if I spend an hour with that person I'm going to find out what's not resolved. I want to create a place where they can come for their own healing. There would be highly trained therapists to work with them. Maybe in an old farmhouse, somewhere peaceful. I'd like to make it a centre of excellence for the study and treatment of Indigenous addictions."

Nel Wieman's vision is equally forward-looking. "We need to acknowledge what's happened historically," she told me during our time together. "But we also need to focus on the solutions and what the future holds. I think that will come from my generation, and even more so from the generation that comes after."

Wieman and Menzies have similar prescriptions for improving their peoples' lives. The first would be streamlining government departments and health agencies so that the care goes where it's needed.

"Aboriginal Corrections may not know what FNIB [First Nations and Inuit Health Branch] is doing, and FNIB may not know what·Indian Affairs is doing," Menzies told me. "Once a First Nations person moves to an urban centre, Ottawa is saying that they are the responsibility of the province. But the province is saying, no, they're not our responsibility, because the *Indian Act* says 'Indian'. So if they could just get rid of all this and say, yeah, we at Indian Affairs are responsible for First Nations, that'd be a big help."

Jurisdictional problems also affect the medical profession. According to Wieman, "In psychiatry no one really wants to deal with addictions. If someone with a substance abuse problem goes to a psychiatrist, they'll be told to get help for their addiction first. Not to say that all my patients with mental health problems have a substance abuse problem, but those who have substance abuse problems also have mental health issues. I think the two are inextricably linked. I want to see an improved mental health status for our people. I would love to see much lower rates of suicide. Policy decisions are based on research, and so far Indigenous people have not been the researchers. I'm doing what I can to better inform Aboriginal mental health and addiction policies."

Wieman also wants more Aboriginal health-care specialists to be trained. "The Royal Commission on Aboriginal Peoples recommended 10,000 health professionals be trained in ten years," she said. "The infrastructure to train that many health professionals just doesn't exist. Try to tell any of the seventeen medical schools in Canada that they need to make training Aboriginal physicians a priority. There are very few schools in Canada that have answered that challenge."

The problems might seem insurmountable to many, but not to these two gifted Aboriginal healers. "Actually, I see a lot of hope for the Aboriginal people," Peter Menzies told me. "Number one, we're the fastest-growing population in Canada. Number two, we're the fastest-growing population in terms of attendance at colleges and universities. Who would have thought that I'd be in Toronto and every month our First Nations newspaper comes to my doorstep and I sit and read it?

Who would have thought that there would be an Aboriginal People's Television Network? So the signs of improvement are all there, but we still have to deal with addictions and mental health issues. We still need to get at the core of the intergenerational trauma."

Sousan Abadian believes Aboriginal people in Canada are paving the way for others. Their advocacy here has led to the residential school settlement (a process of redress that hasn't taken place yet in the United States) and the creation of the Aboriginal Healing Foundation, which has funded many successful and creative healing strategies. "I think we're learning a lot from Indigenous people in Canada. I think they're on the forefront. Economists and others in international development will become aware of these experiments, because we've never talked about what trauma is, let alone about healing from it. So now we have language for it, and we're becoming conscious of it. What do we do about this? At Alkali Lake, I learned it often starts with just a few people in the community becoming sober, becoming denumbed. They start to feel their emotions and start to work through their suffering and pain. Over time, they start a process for their whole community."

Nel Wieman reflects the same kind of commitment. She is always on call when her people need her, even touring Aboriginal schools as part of a mentorship program.

"We're taught that we need to use the gifts we've been given as best we can and work as hard as we can over the course of our lifetime to make things better, for our young people especially," she told me. "That's a huge responsibility, but that's really who we are as Indigenous people. I see myself as a product of seven generations past where things have happened that allow me to become who I am today. The full impact of what I accomplish in my lifetime will not be realized for seven generations, but I want to see an improved mental health status and health status for our people. I want to see that gap closed. And I truly hope that there is a much more positive status quo for Indigenous people, not just in Canada but all over the world, as soon as possible."

Moving from Pain to Hope

MY FIRST VISIT TO DAVIS INLET IN 1979 WAS INTENDED AS a pleasure trip on board the HMV *Bonavista,* which took passengers and supplies up and down the Labrador coast. An adventurous Danish friend named Jutte Selnu came with me to birdwatch. I was eager to see the two Aboriginal cultures of the Labrador coast, the Innu and the Inuit. The little CN coastal boat slowly made its way along the Labrador Sea, stopping in small fishing communities along the way. There were some Innu people travelling on the vessel who slept in an overhang at the front of the boat—the steerage compartment. I was told this was all they could afford, though I later came to believe racist policy explained the situation. Jutte and I shared a cabin with a young Inuit woman from Nain, but none of the Aboriginal passengers were allowed to eat in the dining room until the non-Aboriginals had been served. Inuit and Innu children peered in through the window at us, obviously hungry as they waited for us to finish. One afternoon an Inuit man named Abel Leo invited me to have supper with him, and I suggested we eat together during the first seating. When he told me this would create problems, I invited him to help me do just that. The waiter asked Mr. Leo to leave the table, but I explained that I needed him to stay since he was paying for my meal. Confused, the waiter didn't push the issue further.

We were advised that the boat's stop at Davis Inlet would be short, and the crew seemed to be preparing themselves for some unpleasantness there. As soon as we docked, Innu children rushed on board. One young boy had a fistful of money, which I later learned was to buy alcohol from crew members who were bootlegging. Jutte and I decided to disembark, though we were warned the boat would be leaving as soon as supplies had been unloaded. Both of us began to cry as we strolled along the dusty roadway. The houses in Davis Inlet were dilapidated and the village unkempt; garbage and sewage were strewn everywhere. There were no adults in sight, and most of the village's children were giving the *Bonavista's* crew a merry chase. I walked into an abandoned house whose front door was hanging off its hinges. The rooms were small. There was a sink in the kitchen, but clearly the house had no running water. It was obvious that this house, like the others around it, had been poorly and hastily constructed. Farther down the road, the graveyard was filled with rows and rows of tiny crosses. The dead were young, and there seemed to be so many for such a small town.

Jutte ran on ahead to the boat when she heard the departure whistle blow. By then, however, I was deep in conversation with a young Innu woman named Katie Rich, who had arrived as part of a small delegation that included a Catholic priest. I had my tape recorder running, and Katie was telling me about the need for new housing in the community. She looked about eighteen, yet clearly a leader already. The crew of the *Bonavista* threatened to leave without me, but Jutte stood on the gang-plank until I made it back on board.

I stayed in touch with Katie Rich and her community after that visit. Small upgrades were made over the years to the housing, but the core issues that created deep despair among her people were not resolved until twenty-three years later, when the federal government finally agreed to relocate the community.

The Mushuau Innu, as the Davis Inlet people call them-selves, are one of Canada's last nomadic people. The houses I saw in 1979 had been built in 1967, the year 400 Mushuau Innu agreed to settle in one place, because their children had been promised quality schooling, good medical care and the amenities southerners enjoyed, principally running water. But none of that was ever delivered to the community. The people were settled on an island, which made it impossible for them to continue the caribou hunt that was their principal economy and the core of many spiritual practices. The island had no adequate fresh water supply, and only non-Aboriginal teachers and the nuns who ran the school were supplied with running water. By 1992, the year six children died in a house fire, a staggering 90 per cent of the community's adults admitted they were alcoholic. By 1999, many of the youth were inhal-ing gas fumes to get high and escape their pain. Only after the plight of the Davis Inlet people made international headlines did the federal government finally act, agreeing to move the community to a mainland site. There, a brand-new commu-nity called Natuashish was created. Seven hundred Mushuau Innu moved from Davis Inlet to Natuashish by snowmobile in the winter of 2002.

In December 2005, I was invited to Natuashish to show the film I'd made about Pien Penashue's canoe. I invited Tshaukuesh to accompany me. We spent one of our days there ice fishing and visiting Tshaukuesh's friends and family.

The natural beauty of Natuashish is striking. Thick stands of tall black spruce trees shelter houses set in a valley. On fine winter days, adults dangle fishing lines below the ice on a large frozen lake while children play hockey. At home, townspeople eat Arctic char, salmon or caribou they have fished or hunted themselves. Everything is new, with an infrastructure that would be the envy of any reserve in Canada.

Drunks aren't as common a sight on the streets of Natuashish as they were in Davis Inlet. Drinking takes place in designated "party" houses, and the drunks emerge only when all the liquor has been consumed. Sometimes people disappear for days.

I didn't see any sign of widespread drinking or solvent use during my 2005 visit. My sleep was disturbed one night, however, by the sound of banging on nearby doors. When I peeked out the window of the house where I was staying, I saw a huddle of people knocking on a front door across the street. No one answered. The group moved away as one, in a strange kind of unison, and repeated their banging at the next house on the street. Once again, they were ignored. This routine continued until the light went on over one door and the group went inside. I told my friend Nympha Byrne what I'd seen the next morning, and she explained the group was probably going door to door looking for more alcohol. People ignore the knocking if they are not drinking themselves, because they don't want the disturbance of having drunks in their homes.

Shortly after Tshaukuesh and I left Natuashish, we learned that a young woman named Debbie Rich had died of exposure the night following our departure. She'd been drinking and had passed out in the extreme cold. I thought about the huddle of people I'd witnessed moving down the street and wondered if Rich had been one of them. She might also have been one of the people in the highly publicized video of 1993 showing Davis Inlet children high on gasoline. Debbie Rich was a thirteen-year-old solvent abuser at the time. Her funeral was held in the school gymnasium, because there was no church in Natuashish at the time.

The frequency of funerals in the community's new school must have made it a somewhat grim place for the children who use it during school hours. (A church was built in 2007.) The graveyard in Natuashish is another reflection of the town's continuing struggle for sobriety. Most of the graves belong to young people who died while drunk or from suicide. Darren Pokue, the eighteen-year-old son of the town's chief, ran into the bush when he was drunk, and his body was not found until months later. No one knew if he had meant to harm himself or simply couldn't make it home to avoid freezing to death.

Alcoholism has created such severe social problems among the Mushuau Innu that the community of Natuashish is supposed to be dry. There's no retail sale of alcohol. But that's only on the surface. Beneath it there's a thriving black market for booze, and nobody seems to know how to stop it. The same situation exists across Canada in many "dry" Aboriginal communities.

Some of the people selling alcohol in Natuashish are non-drinkers. They hold down jobs and so can afford the cost of a flight to the nearest liquor store, 275 kilometres south in Goose Bay. If you're a heavy drinker in Natuashish (and it's black or white here—either total abstinence or drunkenness), you depend on others to supply the fix. While there's no law preventing people from bringing in a drink for themselves, the sale of alcohol is not permitted.

"The bootleggers are what we call dry drunks," Debbie's cousin Joyce Rich explained when I telephoned after learning of Debbie's death. "They don't care how they're hurting people."

Ron Snow, who manages the government-owned liquor store in Goose Bay, knows how liquor is getting into Natuashish. "Distillers are using plastic instead of glass these days," he told me, pointing to the rows and rows of whiskey bottles that line his shelves. "I guess that makes it easy for people to hide it in their suitcases. We sell a lot of flasks and 60-ounce bottles of hard liquor here."

Selling smuggled alcohol is lucrative. A hip flask of whiskey goes for $50; 1.8 litre bottles run from $350 to $800 when supplies are low. Beer is much harder to hide in luggage, so it's not brought in. Hard liquor is a quicker way to inebriation anyway, but it's more dangerous. It certainly was for Debbie Rich.

One man who flies frequently between Goose Bay and Natuashish is rumoured to be a bootlegger. In a conversation we had at the airport, he admitted he used to sell liquor, but said he doesn't do it any more. "I just did it when I was laid off from my job. That was six months ago," he told me.

George Gregoire Sr., who works for the Natuashish band council, also frequently flies to Goose Bay. Gregoire told me he too used to bring in alcohol for sale. He and his wife, Charlotte, are now sober, but since some of their children are not, the Gregoires must raise their grandchildren. It's a vicious cycle for many people.

His own parents didn't object, Gregoire told me, when George had his first drink of home brew at the age of sixteen.

Binge drinking wasn't such a problem then; people still lived in the bush, and they would have frozen or starved to death if alcohol had become a big part of their lives.

"My father and mother seemed to be proud of me," Gregoire, now in his sixties, told me in his home, noisy from the activities of his six grandchildren, all under the age of ten. "They offered me more to drink. Well, it seems like they thought I was an adult, and I felt like an adult after drinking. Afterwards I had a very bad headache, and I thought never again would I drink alcohol. But when I got back to the community, I drank again. When they started to sell beer and alcohol in Goose Bay, I drank more. I felt like an adult even though I was just a teenager. I thought it was okay. My parents didn't mind my drinking. I'd have a drink with friends, and I liked the way I felt. I wasn't shy. I could say anything I wanted to say. I wasn't afraid to talk to friends or any girls in the community."

Gregoire spent forty years drinking heavily, trying abstinence off and on but losing the battle until he nearly died from drinking. "Why did I have to drink every day, every day?" he wondered aloud. "Other people, they could drink once a day and stop. I had to keep on drinking. It's a good question why I kept on drinking. I still had no education then. Like some people, I was ashamed. I was the one who forced Charlotte, my wife, to drink. She started to drink and she wanted to keep on and she drank every day until she became an alcoholic. The last time I ended up in hospital in Goose Bay the doctor told me, 'George, I've been looking at your hospital record, and most of it is alcohol-related sickness.' It is a community problem here, not an individual problem. The community needs to get together. Every single family has to get together, to work together, be nice to each other. We need to have a big meeting, without any outsider, just Innu people—former leaders, the former councillors, the Innu nation and the health commission. Get together, and some of the young teenagers who are doing good, invite them to the meeting, and let's talk about how to help our community, because people are against each other and feel miserable about what people did to each other. They're against each other because of money."

The cash economy has created a lot of tension within Innu communities, because it has dramatically disrupted the social order. The Innu once shared everything they had, and no one tried to accumulate riches. When I asked a friend in Sheshatshiu as late as the mid-1980s why no Innu person operated a taxi service or store, she explained, "If someone needed food or a ride and didn't have the money to pay, we'd give them what they needed anyway." There are very strong strictures in hunting societies against hoarding food or tools, because that can mean life or death. The cash economy has complicated peoples' relationships and created terrible fractures in communities that desperately need to work together to restructure.

Every single person in Natuashish suffers from searing personal pain as the result of an alcohol-related family tragedy. Yet Sergeant Grant Smith of the RCMP detachment in Natuashish says there's nothing his officers can do about the illegal sale of alcohol. Even if bootleg liquor is discovered, charges won't be laid, because a few years ago someone was acquitted after successfully arguing that the large quantity of alcohol found in his suitcase was for personal consumption. The band council needs to pass a bylaw making it illegal to bring in any alcohol at all, Smith told me. That bylaw has been promised for some time, but Joyce Rich was not optimistic anything would be done when I spoke to her in 2005. At that time, the band council rarely held public meetings. Chief Simon Pokue had been undergoing grief counselling and addiction treatment at the Poundmaker's Lodge in Alberta in 2004 when all hell broke loose following press reports that $3 million was missing from Natuashish community funds. Pokue cut short his treatment to deal with the mess, and he told me in an interview that he'd been off and on the bottle ever since.

In a referendum held in Davis Inlet in 1998, 60 per cent of the townspeople supported a ban on consumption of alcohol in the community. Pokue told me he didn't think a ban was a reasonable option, since many addicts would not be able to go cold turkey if alcohol suddenly disappeared. Anyway, do bans really work? he questioned. Pokue told me the band council was supposed to find out on a visit to Old Crow, a Yukon reserve, where there is an alcohol ban, but there was no money to make the trip.

Ironically, there is already a community not far from Natuashish where alcohol is banned. Employees at INCO's Voisey's Bay mine site are routinely searched for alcohol and drugs when they fly into the campsite. Infractions result in job loss. It seems easier to protect mine property from the ravages of alcohol abuse than it is to protect people. The proud abstainers of Natuashish hope reform will come one person at a time. But they want the bottles taken away first. And so does the man driving solutions for Aboriginals in Australia.

Seeking Solutions Down Under

PALM ISLAND IS A TROPICAL PARADISE NEAR THE GREAT Barrier Reef in northeastern Australia. It is also, with a population of 3,500, both home to the largest Aboriginal community on that continent and, according to the *Guinness Book of World Records,* the "most likely place in which to die young." During one eight-month period in 2003, there were sixteen youth suicides and eight murders, according to a government report. There's one house for every seventeen people and enough jobs for just 5 per cent of the population. Most of the adults on Palm Island are addicted to drugs and alcohol.

Colonial authorities used Palm Island as a penal colony for Aboriginal people for many years. In the early part of the twentieth century, Noel Pearson's great-grandfather spent his life avoiding Australian police; they were trying to deport him to Palm Island because he had taken up arms to defend his people's territory from gold miners. Had his great-grandfather been captured, Noel Pearson would have been raised on the island rather than in the safe enclave of a Lutheran mission near Cookstown. And he might never have had the opportunity to develop and implement his ideas for stopping the cycle of Aboriginal addiction and violence that Australian policy makers are watching with such interest today. Pearson, at forty-three, has already lived longer than the average Palm Island citizen. Life expectancy there is only forty—a good thirty years less than the Australian national average.

During my research for this book, story after story on Aboriginal addiction and dysfunction in Australia arrived in my electronic mailbox. Media reports presented a picture of communities in great distress. Then one day I came across the transcript of an interview the Australian Broadcasting Corporation had done several years earlier with Noel Pearson. "Some of the poor thinking is such that Aboriginal people believe that it is Aboriginal to drink," Pearson told interviewer Paul Barclay, "and when you get to the stage where a people actually believe that it is somehow part of their identity that we live in parks, that we sit around in circles and drink, that we sit around and waste all of our money in gambling and stuff—when you get people to that state of mind, or where they actually believe that it's to identify as a true Aboriginal person to engage in those things, I think that's a real indication of how wrong the whole tone and the whole direction of thinking about Aboriginal people in this country has become."

Pearson acknowledged to Barclay that he is a controversial figure, known for saying some unpopular things. Like this: "It sounds terribly conservative and terribly old-fashioned to talk about the fact that we've got to restore work, and work was part of our traditional life, you know, a huge part of our traditional life. It was harder work than it is living in this modern society, and yet we tend to think that Aboriginal people and work are somehow foreign to each other."

Pearson's points sounded persuasive, especially when he talked about the bureaucratic control of Aboriginal lives. His words captured something I had heard many Aboriginal people in Canada express. "We are inmates of an institution, an historical institution, these communities; and these communities can be really debilitating of individual endeavour and family responsibility. I think that we've got to break out of those bureaucratic structures and create more room, more freedom for people to take up opportunities and solve problems. Those are the two things we've got to do: seize opportunities, solve problems," he told Barclay.

I scheduled an interview with Pearson in October 2006. I was in a radio booth in St. John's while he sat in a makeshift studio in Cairns, a city of 120,000 on the east coast of the Cape York Peninsula. (The local Australian Broadcasting studio was being renovated.) The peninsula is home to 15,000 Aboriginal people, he told me.

According to Pearson, the Lutheran-run mission where he was raised by his parents provided shelter from the "violent and uncaring" frontier mentality of invading gold miners and a "rapacious colonial society." He earned scholarships to university and eventually law school. Today he dedicates his life to improving social conditions for his people. He has been branded a right-winger for the solutions he proposes, but three Australian Aboriginal communities are putting his solutions to work, with the support of the federal government. It's an ambitious social experiment that attempts to undo the horrifying amount of damage wreaked in just a few short decades.

"I was a young boy when the government still had the power to remove people from our community to Palm Island," Pearson told me. "It was used as a punishment island, a place to remove dissenters and recalcitrants. Palm Island is the concentrated legacy of the grim history of arbitrary government action."

The problems of addiction, suicide and sexual abuse that have given Palm Island its reputation as one of the most dangerous places on earth are found in many other Australian Aboriginal communities, to varying degrees. In fact, the social disintegration of Aboriginal society generates some of the country's most sensational news headlines.

"The Australian Land Where Petrol Fuels Nothing but Despair," cried the 2005 headline for a story in the *Australian* about a place where Aboriginal children and adults inhale gas fumes on a regular basis. Solvent abuse is such an acute problem in Australia's Aboriginal communities that British Petroleum has developed a fouler-smelling gasoline called Opal to make the practice of inhaling gas less attractive. The Australian federal government subsidizes its sale in Aboriginal areas.

The Australian Broadcasting Corporation ran a story the same year under the headline "Brain-Damaged Men Imprisoned without Crime"; it told of two Aboriginal men whose substance abuse had made them mentally ill and violent. "Army Won't Fight Indigenous Violence," reported the Sydney *Morning Herald* in May 2006, after a politician suggested that using the military "to address the national disaster of child abuse and domestic violence in some remote communities should not be ruled out." "Aboriginal Boys Sexually Abused," trumpeted a headline in the fall of 2006 in Melbourne's *The Age*. The line "One in 10 Indigenous Men Raped" headed a story about a survey conducted by the Queensland University of Technology.

The words used to describe the problems in Aboriginal Australian communities are different from those used in Canada—people sniff "petrol," detox centres are called "sobering-up centres" and beer is known as "grog"—but many of the problems are the same. As in Canada, Australian Aboriginals date the social disintegration of their communities to the 1950s and '60s. Things started going downhill in Noel Pearson's community at Hopevale when he was approaching his teens in the mid 1970s.

"I saw what happened to the social norms," Pearson said, "because my parents and their generation would not tolerate someone drinking in their home or coming into their home drunk. I saw those social norms challenged by the young men who achieved capitulation through violence."

Pearson avoided getting involved in what he calls "binge-drinking circles" because he was at university, isolated from most of his peers. He returned to his community an educated man and an activist. Initially he believed that once the legal recognition of his peoples' land rights was achieved, their social problems would go away.

"The first ten years of my work was in pursuit of the land rights of our people," he told me. "We succeeded in getting many land claims through negotiation and through legal claims, but by the end of the 1990s there was an emerging argument in Australia that land rights had not delivered any solutions for Aboriginal people. The social condition of our people had not improved and was going backwards."

Pearson's search for solutions was aided by Anestasia Shkilnyk's book, *A Poison Stronger than Love*. "I was really very much galvanized by that book when I read it in the '80s," Pearson said, "and it caused me to reflect on the condition of our communities in North Queensland."

Shkilnyk wrote the book after doing a stint on contract for the Department of Indian and Northern Affairs in 1976.

She had been sent in to develop programs to help the people of Grassy Narrows recover from the massive mercury spill in their river system, but what she found was a community in chaos from widespread alcohol abuse.

"In the day care centre where I lived," she writes, "I could not help but be exposed to the difficulties this caused, because battered women and abandoned children came there to seek warmth, refuge, and food."

There were eleven deaths by violence the first year Shkilnyk was there, amid a population of 500. She spent almost three years on the reserve, and the suffering she witnessed so troubled her that she spent another year poring over government documents in search of solutions. She learned that between 1959 and 1963, 91 per cent of deaths at Grassy Narrows had been due to natural causes. In the space of a single decade, those numbers had changed dramatically; by the mid-1970s, 77 per cent of deaths on the reserve were alcohol-related. During that time, the people of Grassy Narrows had been relocated from a reserve where they had a subsistence economy to one where the soil was too poor to garden. The mercury, which came from a pulp and paper mill, had destroyed their fishing and guiding economy.

"Probation officers in Kenora said they had no trouble with people at Grassy Narrows until the government moved them to the new reserve," Shkilnyk writes. On the old reserve, she says in her book, families had practised naming ceremonies, puberty vision quests and responsibility ceremonies for their children. All of these customs had come under attack by residential schools and the Christian church, and in 1977, when federal funds poured into the reserve, a social welfare system replaced family responsibilities. Grassy Narrows soon had the highest number of children in foster care in the region.

"What government policy has accomplished is to push the Indian people farther away from participation in the productive activities of the nation," Shkilnyk writes. "What struck me about Grassy Narrows was the numbness in the human spirit. There was an indifference, a listlessness, a total passivity that I could neither understand nor seem to do anything about. I had never seen such hopelessness anywhere in the Third World."

"What Shkilnyk said about Grassy Narrows differing so profoundly from some of the most deprived places in the Third World really struck a chord with me," Pearson explained, "because she could well be describing my communities here in northern Australia. There is a more profound problem than one of material poverty."

The profound problem, Pearson thinks, is what he calls "passivity." He spat the word out during our conversation with marked fervour.

"The book really got me thinking about the role that passive welfare has played in destroying any sense of responsibility. It has eroded and corroded the fabric of our community. My parents and grandparents were people who took responsibility for their families. There'd be absolutely no question about that, whereas today the achievement has been tragically unravelled," Pearson said. "If we don't tackle passivity as a behavioural problem, then I think our culture will continue to unravel."

Pearson's own book, *Our Right to Take Responsibility*, was published in 2000. In it, he challenges Aboriginal Australians to take back the care of their communities and redress policies that have given their people the shortest life expectancy in the world, high prison incarceration rates and a very low percentage of post-secondary graduates.

"My father and grandfather and uncles had been actively involved in economic life, mainly in the cattle industry," he said during our interview. "In the 1970s our human and land rights started to be recognized. But a number of deleterious things happened at the same time: the cattle industry failed and the government made social security available as an alternative source of livelihood. The pubs were opened up to our people. We had young men exposed to idle time, free money and access to the pubs. The alcohol problem started to gather pace, first with the young men, then grew to engulf other segments of our community; women never drank until the eighties. The problem just kept snowballing, and once you've got young women involved in the binge-drinking circles, then you have the fetal alcohol problems."

Pearson's book created a firestorm of controversy, with accusations that he was blaming the victims and was wrong to target welfare dependency. But since its publication, he is getting a chance to put his theories to the test. Today he leads the Cape York Institute for Policy and Leadership based in Cairns. Pearson's institute, whose mission statement is "to enable the people of Cape York to have the capabilities to choose a life that they have reason to value," has already accomplished some very impressive things. Pearson has attracted business donors who pay for Aboriginal children to attend Australian private schools; they are supported by Aboriginal mentors in the hope that they will return home and take on leadership roles in their communities. In 2007 one of Pearson's protégés, Tania Major, was chosen Australia's young person of the year. Pearson has partnered with an Australian bank that provides free counselling services to Aboriginal people on budgeting and saving money. And three communities on the Cape York peninsula, including Pearson's hometown, Hope Vale, have agreed to participate in an ambitious welfare reform experiment. The federal government has passed the necessary legislation to allow the communities to opt out of the national welfare system; receipt of welfare by individuals will now be tied to the social norms Pearson says must be re-established.

"We consider school attendance prima facie, and neglect of the welfare of the child means income support will be redirected towards another responsible family member or through another agency," he told me. "These decisions will be made by a Families Commission, which will be chaired by a retired magistrate with two elders from the community. This commission will make decisions about the reallocation of welfare support, so that we get parents and other adults to fulfill their obligations for the welfare of children."

An "alcohol management plan" makes it illegal to consume grog (alcohol) at home or anywhere else in the three communities. "Keeping alcohol and binge-drinking circles out of the homes and out of the villages has achieved the most positive results," Pearson reported.

He expected some opposition from the tourism industry, he said, but what most dismayed Pearson was the opposition he got from non-Indigenous employees in Aboriginal communities. "The people who were most intimately acquainted with the nature of the problem in these communities—the teachers who didn't have kids in their classrooms, the nurses who dealt with the broken bones, the policemen who pick up the drunks—their ability to have wine and beer in their fridges was a greater imperative than trying to tackle this raging social problem," he said.

Pearson does get discouraged sometimes. "It's really the Grassy Narrows question," he told me. "How it is that addiction and misaligned incentives can destroy love? It's the most depressing thing that I see: the people who love their children very much—and you can see it in the way they indulge their children—yet they act in ways that could not be more calculated to be detrimental. I've seen so many people act in ways that are destructive of the interests of their children." Pearson seems a warm but forceful man, determined to give his people the chance to pick up where his parents' generation left off. Theirs was a generation that prided itself on survival through even tougher times.

"We live in an era when the level of hostility and racism has been reduced," Pearson said. "The opportunities are much greater than anything that passed by the door of my parents or earlier generations, yet our young people today are less able to take advantage of opportunity than previous generations, simply because we have embedded dysfunction within our communities."

Pearson is sympathetic to the arguments advanced in Canada and elsewhere that colonial policies and intergenerational trauma create the conditions that give addiction its hold on Aboriginal people. He knows this is true. It's not enough, though, to have this understanding.

"There is an historical explanation for why we're in the miserable condition that we're in," Pearson said, "but that by itself doesn't provide a solution. Sorry, but I'm not convinced there's a great therapeutic solution that the engineers of social justice are somehow going to deliver to us at some great moment in our history. It's just not going to happen. My grandparents' generation suffered huge traumas as young children, and yet they are an example of people having rebuilt lives out of terrible trauma. The trauma we have now is the trauma of addiction epidemics that have simply got out of control. The people who are engaged in this dysfunctional lifestyle today don't have the same excuse my grandfather had in terms of their traumatic histories. In fact, many of the people today engaged in substance abuse and destroying the prospects of their children were brought up in good homes. We've got to confront. We've got to be honest about these problems, and I think an honest confrontation is the starting point for change."

Change is being made slowly as Pearson waits for Australia's central government to pass the legislation he needs to carry out his solutions. A new government was elected in Australia in 2007, and Pearson has expressed some fears he may not have its full support. Even without full government support, however, it's hard to imagine Noel Pearson ever backing away from the movement he has started.

Heartache in Kenora

A MOVING STORY PUBLISHED IN THE *KENORA MINER* IN
the fall of 2005 described a vigil held on World Suicide Prevention Day, September 10, at the Kenora waterfront. Chief Arnold
Gardiner made a connection between youth suicide and alcohol abuse when he spoke to the people who had gathered. One
of the reserves in the area, Whitefish Bay, had had ten youths
die by suicide in the space of just a year and a half. Suicide was
so frequent, in fact, that the fourteen reserves around Kenora
and the forty-nine reserves north of and surrounding Thunder
Bay had declared a state of emergency.

The vigil's organizer was Tania Cameron, then program
manager of Aboriginal Healing and Wellness for the Kenora
Chiefs Advisory. The KCA provides services to seven adjacent
First Nations reserves. In addition to holding down a full-time
job when I met her in May 2006, Cameron was also complet-
ing courses at Winnipeg's Red River College in First Nations
governance, raising two young children and serving as a band
council member for her own reserve of Dalles.

Cameron had to cancel our first meeting due to a suicide on the Wabaseemoong (Whitedog) reserve. The victim was in her mid-twenties, a young woman with two young daughters. She had been suffering from depression since her sister's suicide a year earlier. The woman's death was not sudden; she had taken an overdose of prescription medicine and then lingered on life support for several weeks. When I checked my e-mail that evening from my Kenora hotel, there was an eerily coincidental one from Allan Saulis of the Maliseet First Nation in Tobique, New Brunswick, with the subject line "Another suicide." Saulis wasn't talking about what had happened at Wabaseemoong that day. He was talking about his hometown.

"There was another suicide this weekend in our community of about 1,500," Saulis wrote. "This will be the third. How many more will it take for the authorities, governments and the media to take affirmative action once and for all?"

No one knows for sure how many Aboriginal people in Canada are dying from suicide each year, because there is no central agency keeping track. Coroners in most provinces do not tabulate suicide by ethnic origin. More than a decade ago, the Royal Commission on Aboriginal Peoples estimated the rate of Aboriginal suicide to be five to six times the Canadian average and recommended the creation of a coordinated national strategy on Aboriginal suicide that would keep track of the number of deaths, conduct research into the causes and fast-track solutions. The Royal Commission felt the issue was so urgent it released an interim report on suicide before its main report was released. Yet their recommendation has still not been followed. In 1999 the Canadian Institute of Child Health estimated that First Nations men between the ages of fifteen and twenty-four kill themselves at the rate of 126 per

100,000, compared with 24 per 100,000 in the general population. The 2005–2006 Senate Committee on Mental Health, Mental Illness and Addiction, led by Michael Kirby, was told the rate of youth suicide in the Sioux Lookout area is 398 per 100,000, compared with the Canadian average of 12.9 per 100,000. It's believed the rates are even higher for Canadian Inuit, who also urged Kirby's committee to recommend urgent action. In the end, the Senate committee called for the creation of a Canadian Mental Health Commission to look for solutions to the suicide crisis and "the alarming alcohol and substance abuse rates in Aboriginal communities." Senator Kirby leads this commission, but it remains to be seen when the Aboriginal problems his committee called "a national disgrace" will be dealt with. There's fear among national Aboriginal organizations that the needs of those outside Aboriginal communities will take precedence over their own citizens' needs.

It's rare to find an Aboriginal person in Canada who has not lost a close friend or relative to suicide. In the absence of a coordinated strategy, people across the country are trying to find solutions on their own. When Tania Cameron became program manager of Aboriginal Healing and Wellness at the age of only twenty-six, she set out to do something about the glaring shortage of mental health and addiction services for the communities around Kenora. She successfully negotiated a deal with Ontario's Ministry of Health and Long Term Care to create a mental health division within the Kenora Chiefs Advisory. Among other things, the deal enabled her to hire Ozzie Seunath, a psychologist, to lead a team of six mental health and addictions workers.

Seunath, an immigrant to Canada from the Caribbean, will never forget his first day on the job in 2003. There'd been a suicide on one reserve, and it was followed by another, then another. "I thought, I don't know how to stop this," he told me when we met in the spring of 2006. "We were rushing in there, making sure the friends and family members were looked after, because when one suicide happened, it was often followed by others, and this used to scare the heck out of us."

Since then, Seunath has learned enough to confidently identify one of the reasons young Aboriginal men and women take their lives.

"What is there for young people to do, in terms of defining economic and individual independence?" he said. "What is there for young people to look forward to, in terms of training and so on? Without that direction and hope for the future, it's easy to sink into 'that's all there is'."

According to Seunath, suicide can also be a drastic way to solve personal problems.

"The young adults put so much emotional energy into their relationships that if they break up, life seems pretty worthless. It's like the worst blow that will ever hit them. But if life had more opportunity, more hope for them and support, then they would see a breakup as a barrier to overcome rather than something to succumb to."

Seunath compares his own experience, as the descendant of slaves growing sugarcane in the Caribbean, with that of Aboriginal Canadians. He says while his people suffered poverty, they were large enough in number to maintain the cultural and spiritual beliefs that sustain emotional resiliency. That's not the case for many of his clients. "The native people had more denial and suppression of their cultural practices and identity," he says. "Because of residential schools, they haven't learned parenting and their traditional ways, so it is very difficult for them to pass on that kind of learning."

Drug and alcohol addiction are the lethal results of this oppression and sense of hopelessness, Seunath believes. Charles McDonald, the community wellness worker for the Wabaseemoong reserve, told me the practice of lacquer sniffing is also damaging young people. "You wouldn't believe how thick the skin grows on the hands of those people who hold rags soaked in lacquer up to their mouths and noses," he said, clearly horrified at what had become a daily occurrence for some on his reserve.

The Whitefish Bay First Nation, six kilometres off the highway that connects Kenora to Sioux Narrows, has one of the most affluent-looking reserves in Canada. There are nice houses, tidy lawns, flower pots hanging from porches and dads pushing children in strollers. Yet in the spring of 2006, an elder and some children designed and mounted a large billboard near the entrance to the reserve. In bold letters it reads: "Bootleggers, We Know Who You Are. Stop Selling Alcohol." The two-storey women's shelter, surrounded by a high fence and protected by security cameras, reflects the violence that alcohol is fuelling.

Seunath says changing things will involve a concerted effort from everyone. "People don't get up and say, I'm going to become a drunk," he told me. "They gradually get into it because of feelings within. Struggles within. The availability of it, and so on. And most of all, a lack of hope and direction. It leads to 'Give it up. Let's just do what feels good at the moment,' basically."

Kenora is a prosperous town with a mainly non-Native population. First Nations residents go to Kenora for all their services, but few people from Kenora go to the reserves. That situation has led to a lot of misunderstanding.

"There has been discrimination based on race over the years," Ozzie Seunath pointed out, "and that is changing slowly. The people from the reserves have been called names that have been destructive to them. They hear accusations that they don't want to work, they don't want to do this. Yet they are not given opportunities for employment, for managing some of their own affairs, that the mainstream is usually given. If that could change, it will build their confidence and create role models for the young people coming up. More opportunities: I see that as key."

The Anishnawbe people who live at Wabaseemoong, two hours north of Kenora, were resettled from three self-sufficient communities in 1958 after an Ontario Hydro industrial project caused massive flooding. Roy McDonald, an elder in Wabaseemoong, vividly recalled how his people, formerly of One Man Lake, learned they were going to be uprooted. He told the story to Brian K. Smith, a former teacher in the community who did some research for the Royal Commission on Aboriginal Peoples. "There was a tent across the river. And a few people were anxious, wanting to know who was out there. So one of my cousins, who was fluent in English, went up to this camp in the afternoon ... and found out they were surveyors. They started to tell him that this land was going to be flooded ... We were forced to relocate. There was never any choice."

The land at Wabaseemoong, given to the people of One Man Lake and those uprooted from other communities, is unsuitable for productive farming. It is also on the same poisoned river as Grassy Narrows. Most of the reserve's public buildings are collapsing today because of the sandy ground upon which they were built. Yet when I spoke to grade twelve students at the reserve's school, they told me they loved their reserve because of the scenery and their close family ties. They knew they'd have to leave to further their education, but all wanted to return to the reserve afterwards. As difficult as reserve life may be, many Aboriginal people consider the reserves to be all they have left of traditional lands and important repositories of language and culture.

Charles McDonald invited me to visit the reserve the day of the young suicide victim's wake. Her body was laid out in a large room inside the band council building. The coffin was covered with flowers, and in a scene of particular poignancy, the dead woman's small daughters sat at a table facing their mother's coffin and played with Barbie dolls. Most others in the room passed the time playing cards in silence.

"The children on the reserve are very quiet today," McDonald explained. "They know that someone has died and, in our culture, there can be no noise or running around. We've lit a sacred fire, and it will burn night and day until the funeral."

Later, the reserve's entire population of 1,200 would gather to share a meal and join a traditional healer to pray for the young woman's soul.

"Suicide is a terrible thing," McDonald said. "We believe that the soul will not leave the earth, and so the healer will try to help."

Despite the devastation the Wabaseemoong reserve had suffered, the feeling of community was strong. Charles told me he had lost one of his children to a rare genetic condition that entailed a long, slow death by physical debilitation. The community had helped his family through the ordeal by leaving extra money on the counter of the family's store after shopping there. That and some well-supported fundraising projects had allowed the family to purchase a special vehicle to transport their son to medical treatments in the United States. The treatments gave their son a better quality of life during his shortened lifetime, and his parents were grateful for that. Charles was repaying his community now with the compassionate services he provided as the wellness worker.

A wellness worker's most harrowing task is being called first to the scene of a suicide. Tania Cameron told me about another wellness worker in her area. "I heard him speak about what he has experienced, going to a home or some place in the community and having to cut down a youth from wherever they are hanging," she said. "And just his description, hearing the pain in his voice. That's his work and he's still, after eleven years, doing that same kind of work. I've just got to give credit or praise for the people who actually do that."

"What kind of toll does it take on him?" I asked.

"When I last saw him," Cameron replied, "he talked about needing to debrief, having to step back and take care of himself. He goes to see someone in Winnipeg for counselling and he takes a few days and then he goes back to work. I see in his eyes and I hear in his voice that he is tired, but you can't stop him. He'll always want to do that."

Charles McDonald sees one solution to the suicide crisis affecting his people: "Give us back what was taken away." In his youth, the fifty-year-old told me, he was never bored. "I used to help my father on the trapline. We picked wild rice and fished, until they started bringing in all kinds of new rules and regulations."

Later that week, in Kenora, Tania Cameron invited me to attend the spring feast held at the Kenora Chiefs Advisory. There, amid generous servings of wild rice, fish and fruit salad, I was introduced to Margaret Quewezance, the grandmother of the young Wabaseemoong suicide victim. Margaret and I sat together while the KCA drum group performed. The lead drummer and singer, T.J. Henry, had a tenor voice to rival any I'd heard before. His soulful singing, the respectful way the drummers followed his cues, and my experiences that week, welled up inside and made me cry. Afterwards, small gifts were presented to everyone, in keeping with the Aboriginal tradition of sharing. There was no indication in the transcendent singer's manner, but the community would suffer a devastating blow months later when T.J. Henry also took his own life.

"I have lost three grandchildren to suicide," Quewezance told me at the feast. "One we just buried yesterday. And right now I'm feeling so emotional, so overwhelmed, mentally and emotionally exhausted. Every time we lose a member to suicide in our community it affects the whole people, in the community and outside the community. I think the contributor to suicide is the lack of knowledge of the traditional way of life, plus the addictions that people are going through nowadays. If there was a way that the bootleggers, these people selling lacquer, could be dealt with. If only our leaders had the guts to say no to lacquer dealing and bootlegging and had more control. The leaders should be enforcing rules outlawing lacquer bootlegging, drugs and alcohol, because there is a lot of that in my community. And the kids are so vulnerable. Some kids are so vulnerable."

Lacquer sniffing, Margaret Quewezance said, is a disturbing way to become intoxicated, yet practised by too many on her reserve. "To me, they appear so withdrawn. And they're really famished, really hungry. A lot of them come to my house looking for food. I think when they are among themselves they will get into pretty nasty fights, but when you encounter one of them on the road or he comes to your house, they seem kind to me, and gentle. I used to live next door to young people who were sniffing, and sometimes late at night I'd come home with my groceries. Somebody would say, 'Kokum [grandmother], do you need help?' And they would help me unpack the car and put everything on the steps and they wouldn't bother me. Sometimes at night I'd hear them yelling: 'Get away from Kokum's house. You stay away from there.' "

Margaret Quewezance grew up at One Man Lake. She remembers a childhood that was economically tough, but in which social norms were intact. Her father, a widower, carried out his responsibilities with the help of the extended family.

"My dad raised three of us, and he took us to cultural events: powwows, shaking tent ceremonies—any kind of ceremony, he would take us. And he would tell us to participate. We did it willingly. And we had the love, support and guidance from the other elders. What my dad couldn't provide for us, my aunts, uncles and grandparents stepped in and helped my dad, because he was raising three children alone."

Margaret's father, who lived to be ninety-eight, had some important advice for his children, advice Margaret told me has been hard to follow in the larger community of Wabaseemoong. "Before he died, my father told us to stick together, love one another. 'Don't let me be the only one that held you together,' he said. 'Go on the way you've been going on.' We haven't been doing that. We're sort of lost. Everybody has drifted apart in their own way."

"And that's happening to a lot of families?" I asked.

"Yep, a lot of families," she said. "I think our leaders should consider forming an elders group and getting their direction from elders. We need to go back to our roots. I think that will be a step in the right direction. I asked a lot of these kids. 'What's your spiritual name?' And they ask, 'What is that?' In the old days, as soon as you were born, you were given a spiritual name to carry you through life. My name is Thunderbird Woman, and I belong to the Sturgeon clan. We all have clanships. I know my children are the Caribou clan, because their dad was the Caribou clan. My dad was the Sturgeon clan, and that's why I'm Sturgeon clan. They say that your clan heals you and your traditional name carries you throughout your life."

"And you'd like the young children to have the same tradition?"

"Yes, I think that would be a big help," she said, "if they went back to their roots."

Tania Cameron also thinks the solution lies in the rebuilding of Anishnawbe pride and cultural awareness. The suicide prevention vigil she helped organize on the Kenora waterfront didn't attract many non-Aboriginals, but a lot of people came in from the reserves.

"There was this large circle of tea lights, reflecting off the water," Cameron told me. "It just breaks your heart to think of them as so many peoples' lives. Their lights were blown out, you know. I try to place my mind where these kids were. It was a place of no hope. I think that's an awful place, for anyone to feel that way."

Cameron said she would like to see more youth exchanges and opportunities for impoverished children on reserves, a sentiment Ozzie Seunath echoed. "If we can have more youth exchanges, educational-type trips, more opportunities for the kids to manage their lives and go in some direction, that would help," he said. "When I see more of that, I'll know we're out of danger. Right now, we can't let our guard down until we see more healthy things happening for the youth. We need to get them into a different mindset so they start feeling good about themselves and their accomplishments."

Progress is being made, Seunath told me, and he feels hopeful that will continue. "What we're seeing right now is actually quite encouraging. We are seeing an increase in First Nations people returning to their cultural roots and reviving customs, language and so on. This will have a positive impact on the identity of the people, especially the young, and this can lead to nothing but good."

Besides returning to her cultural roots, Tania Cameron also believes it's important to ensure that Aboriginal perspectives are brought into mainstream politics. In late 2007 she sought, and won, the NDP nomination for Kenora, and she will run as that party's candidate in the next federal election. She hopes non-Aboriginals in that part of Ontario are ready to embrace an Aboriginal candidate. She hopes too that more non-Aboriginals will join the next World Suicide Prevention Day vigil she organizes on the Kenora waterfront. She'll keep organizing them, she told me, until they're no longer needed.

Addiction, Violence and the Threat to Inuit Women

LAVINIA PIERCEY WAS PASSING A NEIGHBOUR'S HOUSE when she heard children screaming. She heard men's voices, too. Once inside the house, she saw a man trying to grab a little girl while the girl's father fought him off.

"He wanted to touch the little girl sexually," Piercey told me. "She was seven but very tiny; she looked like she was four."

Piercey knew the potential assailant. She's the receptionist at the RCMP detachment in Nain, an Inuit community in Nunatsiavut (Labrador), and the man had been arrested before. According to Piercey, this was not an exceptional example of the violence and chaos she regularly sees in the town of 1,500. Recently, she had heard a friend screaming as she neared the friend's house. "He's hurt, he's hurt," her friend hysterically repeated. When Piercey got inside the house, she found her friend's husband dead on the floor. He'd shot himself while his children watched. Piercey has overheard some of the officers at the RCMP detachment compare what is happening in Nain with what's going on in Hopedale, a nearby community.

"They say domestics are different in Nain. Women in Hopedale get black eyes. In Nain, people are out to kill each other," Piercey told me.

Some Inuit women are speaking publicly about the high rates of violence and sexual abuse in their communities. Their concerns are expressed in a 2006 report called "National Strategy to Prevent Abuse in Inuit Communities." It was prepared by Pauktuutit, the national organization representing Inuit women. "Some community leaders believe that violence has become so destructive to women, children, family relationships and community health that it threatens the very future of the Inuit," the report says.

Canada's Inuit are a national treasure. Their art and artifacts grace our galleries and museums. The inukshuk (a stone structure shaped like a person with outstretched arms) is a Canadian icon. Yet the future of Inuit culture, shaped by the world's coldest weather, is compromised not only by violence and addiction but also by climate change. The Inuit are a tiny minority in this country. Population estimates range from 46,000 to 55,000, the size of a small Canadian town. An estimated 5,000 Inuit live in Ontario towns and cities. Most Inuit live in fifty-three communities spread out over 4,000 kilometres, from Nain in the east to the Northwest Territories. The majority live in Nunavut, the largest of four Inuit territories in Canada.

In Nunavut, the number of women who report having been abused by a spouse is 6.5 times the national average. Statistics Canada reported in 2006 that women in Nunavut used emergency shelters ten times more than women elsewhere in Canada. In a 2006 report entitled "Measuring Violence

Against Women," Statistics Canada noted the number of women killed by their spouses in Nunavut and the Northwest Territories was 7.3 per 100,000, compared to 1 per 100,000 in all of Canada. Pauktuutit believes the spousal abuse rate is as high in other Inuit territories, but because there are only twelve shelters serving Canada's Inuit communities, the statistical picture is incomplete. To whom do you report abuse if there is no women's shelter or RCMP detachment in your community? Inuit women say the isolation of their communities makes it easy for other Canadians to ignore the terrible reality of their sexual and physical abuse. Leesie Naqitarvik helped prepare the Pauktuutit strategy, and she says addiction to drugs or alcohol is one of the root causes of the violence. "The loss of culture, dependence, breakdown of families, denial and mistrust are other causes," she adds.

Jennifer Dickson, the executive director of Pauktuutit, calls the shortage of addiction treatment and mental health services for Inuit appalling. There are very few safe places for women and children who are being abused, and even women who leave an abusive spouse end up returning because they have nowhere else to go. Inuit people live in the most overcrowded houses in Canada. In the Nunavik region, population 10,000, a staggering 500 families are on a waiting list for a home of their own. Home ownership is out of the question for most, because it's so expensive to build houses in the far North; permafrost makes it impossible to put in conventional water and sewer services, and building materials must be shipped up from the South during a short construction season. People rent social housing instead, but that's not keeping pace with the demand, especially as the number of new Inuit families is growing at a very fast rate. The average age for Inuit people is twenty, compared with thirty-seven for Canada as a whole, and 60 per cent of Inuit are under the age of thirty. Inuit are having twice as many babies as most other Canadians.

According to Lavinia Piercey, alcohol addiction is Nain's biggest problem. People drink at the hotel year round, she told me, but the chaos gets worse when the ice breaks up and ships restock the beer store. That's when the cells start to fill at the RCMP detachment. Piercey can describe the drinking culture in her community because she's been part of it. It starts with a few beers at home, she says, then people go to the hotel bar, where they connect with friends. Someone offers to host a house party, where the drinking continues into the early hours of the next day. There's sexual promiscuity, fighting, people passing out.

A study by the National Aboriginal Health Organization's Ajunnginiq Centre says many Inuit avoid alcohol completely. Abstinence rates are higher than the Canadian average, and there are also Inuit who drink moderately. But approximately 40 per cent of Inuit who do drink alcohol consume five or more drinks at a time. Statistics Canada's 2001 report "Family Violence in Canada" states that the spouse of a binge drinker is more likely to be abused than that of a moderate drinker. Aboriginal women are three times more likely to be abused than any other women in Canada, because binge drinking is the drinking style in their communities. The abuse they suffer is also more violent. "Overall, Aboriginal victims were more likely to be either beaten, choked, threatened with a gun or knife, or sexually assaulted," states a report prepared by the Canadian Centre for Justice Statistics in 2005. Lavinia Piercey's ex-husband was a weekend binge drinker. He didn't hurt her, she said, but she and her daughters frequently took refuge in one of the bedrooms to watch TV because they were bothered by the noise when her ex-husband was joined by friends.

Mary Simon, the president of Canada's national Inuit organization, the Inuit Tapiriit Kanatami, told an audience of 3,000 at the Healing Our Spirit Worldwide conference that her people need to make healing a priority, because of the escalating incidence of suicide and drug abuse. She says the trauma her people have suffered over the years is to blame. "There have been many events that caused significant changes in Inuit lifestyles," she told conference delegates, "most of it within the past fifty to a hundred years. We went from nomadic self-sufficient family camps to being moved, sometimes without consent, into permanent settlements with much larger and unfamiliar social structures. Epidemics took a terrible toll. Many lost their lives, while many others were left orphaned and dependent on others for their very survival." Many Inuit in Nain are the descendants of people who the federal government forcibly relocated from islands where they'd been self-sufficient to places where they live a life of welfare dependence. Many Inuit across the North were also pulled from their communities during a tuberculosis epidemic in the 1950s. Because the sick lived in nomadic camps or settlements and had names that were hard for southerners to record, many of them were never returned home, remaining in southern institutions. At a spring 2006 gathering of Inuit addiction and mental health workers in Ottawa, one woman told the group she'd recently found an aunt in a Montreal psychiatric hospital. The first thing her aunt requested was to taste some of the traditional foods she had missed and been unable to get for decades.

Meeka Arnakaq, a Nunavut elder, used a metaphor at the Ottawa gathering to explain why she feels so many Inuit men are angry and frustrated: "If the sled is toppled over, it cannot go. The man is underneath. This is how Inuit men are today. They are stuck. Their responsibilities have been taken away. Who is going to stand them up? We've found different ways of healing women, but not the men. The *qamutik* [sled] has to stand up. The dogs have to start running."

Inuit women, like their First Nations and Metis counterparts, are on the frontline of this crisis, because they provide most of the social services in their communities. The addiction and mental health workers, meeting in Ottawa for the first time together, complained about burnout, but they demonstrated a remarkable commitment to being agents of change. Organizers tried to bolster morale with inspirational talks and group activities, including a word association game. But the women's answers to the question of "what Inuit feel today" demonstrated that the pall in their communities is never far from their minds. Among the negative words recorded on a flip chart were anger, frustration, rejection, humiliation, racism, domination, vengeance, jealousy, isolation, scared, insignificant, worthless, oppressed and suicidal.

Jack Anawak, Canada's Ambassador to Circumpolar Affairs in 2006 (the federal government has since abolished the position, to the dismay of national Inuit organizations), grew up in Repulse Bay, Nunavut, at the time Inuit children were sent to residential school.

"It was not a very good period, in the late '60s and up to the late '70s," he told me. "Young men suddenly lost their role as people who hunted. If you weren't successful in hunting, you starved. All of a sudden that role was taken away by the introduction of store-bought foods. It was devastating for them."

Two of Anawak's brothers died from suicide.

Lavinia Piercey told me there have been so many suicides in Nain that residents are becoming almost numb to it. Her ex-husband recently had lost a niece (aged twenty) and a nephew (aged eighteen), and she was concerned he was drinking to cope with the loss.

"You have to keep very busy," she said, "or drink, to deal with all the terrible things that are happening."

Their high suicide rate (approximately three times the Canadian average according to the Royal Commission on Aboriginal Peoples 1997) is one of the reasons Inuit men have a much shorter lifespan than other Canadian men. As with First Nations men on reserves, their life expectancy is sixty-two years of age, compared with seventy-five for men in the rest of the country. Inuit women live to be seventy-one on average, compared with the average of eighty-two years for Canadian women as a whole.

Leesie Naqitarvik travels across the North to help communities put Pauktuutit's plan for ending abuse into action. She asks local governments to pass zero tolerance resolutions for drugs and alcohol, to set up abuse prevention committees and to sponsor prevention programs. "Land claims organizations can name abuse as a top-priority social and economic issue. Governments can work with Inuit in setting abuse prevention and spending priorities," Pauktuutit's report recommends. The report includes a guide called "Sharing Knowledge, Sharing Wisdom," which provides a concrete plan for organizations, governments and communities themselves to follow in implementing change.

Pauktuutit is trying to tear down the culture of abuse that has grown up to replace what was destroyed by Canada's assimilation policies. Inuit women are lobbying all levels of government for funding to improve addiction and mental health services, and they want the Canadian public to support them. Kevin Lane is the program manager for the Saputjivik treatment centre in Northwest River, Labrador. When I spoke to him in 2006, he was frustrated that Health Canada could provide $130,000 for capital renovations to the building, but no money to train his staff or do community education programs.

If Pauktuutit's strategy to reduce violence is to have any impact at all, it must break through the denial in Inuit communities about the extent of the problem and individual responsibility for it.

As Lavinia Piercey told me, people who want to stop drinking must overcome the embarrassment of others knowing they are seeking treatment. Many lack confidence in the treatment services that do exist, because so many people return to the community and take up drinking again. People in Nain are also punished socially for not drinking, she told me. When Piercey's ex-husband stopped for nine months a few years ago, the family lost all its friends. No one came to visit.

The Inuit government of Nunatsiavut, realizing there were too few rewards for sober residents, applied to the government of Newfoundland and Labrador for help. In 2006, the province provided $78,000 for eight projects intended to reduce violence in Inuit communities. Piercey's community received a small portion of the money to "celebrate those people who have abstained from drug or alcohol consumption for three years or more." This will be done through a retreat-style workshop, with the hope the individuals who participate will become active agents of change for their communities. It's not a lot for such a big problem, but the Inuit have always been ingenious in the way they use their limited resources. They're determined to draw from their heroic past to create a healthier future for their children.

At the Healing Our Spirit conference in Edmonton, Mariam Aglukkaq from Gjoa Haven symbolically lit the *qulliq*, a lamp essential for Inuit survival, before a crowd of thousands from around the world who want to create change in their communities.

Closed-circuit cameras broadcast her actions on two giant screens. With the flourish of a cooking show host, she poured seal oil into a soapstone bowl, then took a small pouch made of caribou skin out of an ingenious purse fashioned from an Arctic loon. There wasn't a sound in the hall as the audience waited for the kindling inside Aglukkaq's pouch to ignite with sparks from the two stones she rubbed together. A puff of smoke soon emerged from the bag, and when Aglukkaq blew air on it, a brilliant blaze of light jumped from the *qulliq*. Pauktuutit hopes its own campaign will ignite a flame in time to protect Inuit women and preserve the beauty of one of Canada's most ancient cultures.

Finding Strength in Inuit Culture

A WOMAN LEANED OUT THE WINDOW OF HER HOUSE and shouted in Inuktitut. Children on their way to school turned around and started running towards the harbour.

"What's going on?" asked Doug Booker, the director of Health Canada's non-prescription drug program. Booker, wearing a heavy Scandinavian-style sweater and toque, was taking pictures of the local church.

"There's a dog team coming back," one of the children called out over her shoulder in English. The team was competing in Ivakkak, the annual dogsled race in its sixth year of operation.

Booker and two companions, also civil servants, joined the children in an excited dash for the harbour at Kangirsuk, a village of 400 Inuit on Ungava Bay in the eastern Arctic. The federal bureaucrats were taking part in the fourth annual Inuit Arctic Tour, an event organized by the Inuit Tapiriit Kanatami, the national organization representing Canada's Inuit.

"The purpose of the tour," explained Stephen Hendrie, ITK's communications director, "is to show senior federal officials the Inuit way of life in a positive manner."

Hendrie had invited me to join the Arctic tour in 2006. That April, sixteen bureaucrats flew with us to Nunavik, a territory the size of France in northern Quebec, 1,500 kilometres north of Ottawa. Here, 10,000 people live in fifteen scattered coastal communities. Previous tours have taken government bureaucrats to Nunavut, Nunatsiavut in Labrador and Inuvialuit communities in the Northwest Territories.

After twenty minutes on the harbour ice, Booker, his colleague, Marie-France LaMarche, and a Department of Fisheries and Oceans official, Danielle Labonte, started to wonder if there'd been a mistake about the dog team's arrival. Their eyes scanned the vast expanse of white for something other than snow and ice. Soon, though, Ivakkak officials stationed themselves near the long string of colourful flags that marked the finish line. Tiny specks of something dark moved closer and closer. With astonishing speed twelve dogs, spread out like a fan, rushed towards the finish, pulling a sled with two men on board.

Mushers Adamie Qurnak and Allie Tukalak were soon surrounded by well-wishers. Bear-shaped men in heavy parkas hugged Qurnak and Tukalak while children stood back, as though in awe of their power. Their team hadn't won, but the two men were happy anyway. This race is about the glory of surviving outdoors in one of the world's harshest climates. It took Qurnak and Tukalak eight days to cross from one end of Nunavik to the other, racing their dogs from Puvirnituq, on the coast of Hudson Bay, east to Kangirsuk: a distance of 525 kilometres. The winning team had made the same trip in five days. As Tukalak emerged from an embrace, I asked him how he was feeling. "I feel like a proud Inuk man," he said. His smile lit up a face burned the colour of mahogany by so many days in the strong spring sun. The mushers hammered poles into the ice to tether their exhausted dogs as Kangirsuk boys hovered, ready to help.

The Arctic tour participants learned more about the importance of the race when we met the officers of Makivik Corporation, the financial backers of Ivakkak and a company unlike any other in Canada. Makivik was established in 1978 with the money Inuit here received as compensation from the James Bay and Northern Quebec hydroelectric project, which caused flooding and water diversion on their land. A $124-million heritage fund was created, and Makivik is in charge of investing that money for the maximum benefit of the Nunavik Inuit.

The president of Makivik is forty-eight-year-old Pita Aatami, an urbane man fluent in English, French and Inukti-tut. From him we learned that successful investments by the corporation have given Inuit mastery over their air space, sea and land. The profits, from the airlines Air Inuit and First Air and a company called Cruise North, have been reinvested in the communities. Ivakkak, the dog team race, is a non-profit venture aimed at building pride. The race is part of a strategy Aatami and his colleagues hope will start cultural renewal and help solve some of the social strife in their homeland. An important part of Inuit culture died when 20,000 Inuit sled dogs were destroyed in the 1960s and '70s. Aatami believes it was a deliberate government policy to keep the Inuit in one place, to prevent them from scattering across their land during the year to hunt and fish. At that time, the federal government was trying to resettle the Inuit into larger communities that would be easier to service. Aatami wants to see an official inquiry into the matter, he told the visiting civil servants. The Inuit here and in Nunavut have been pressing for an inquiry for several years. Most of the official records about what happened have been lost, and the Inuit leadership is not satisfied with an RCMP internal investigation that concluded only diseased dogs were killed.

"We have elders who remember very clearly what happened," Aatami said. "They were afraid to resist, even though they could not understand why their dogs were killed by Quebec police and the RCMP. We believe the dogs were killed so our people would be easier to control."

It's a harsh accusation, and one that reflects the bitterness felt here against Canada for other policies that have damaged Inuit life and made the people economically dependent on the South.

Alcohol, drug abuse, high rates of suicide and family violence are the legacy of rapid cultural change in the North. The report released in 2006 by Pauktuutit, the Inuit women's organization, is not the only one to document the enormity of the problem. Researchers from L'Université de Québec à Trois Rivières have released preliminary results from a survey on alcohol and drug use in Nunavik that indicates 43 per cent of the youth and adults abuse these substances. Alcohol for home use in Nunavik must be shipped north from Montreal, since it can't be purchased in villages, and in 2005 Kuujjuaq's drinkers—from a total of 2,000 people living in the town—spent $1 million on alcohol.

Alcohol and drugs were not part of the feast and ceremony held to celebrate the achievements of the Ivakkak dog team racers. Hundreds of people gathered in the Kangirsuk recreation centre to celebrate the fifteen teams that participated. Air Inuit flew the mushers' wives and children in from neighbouring villages to take part. Medals and prizes were awarded to everyone who survived the rigours of travelling by dog team for days in the bitter cold. Outside the building, though, there were clusters of inebriated young Inuit men. I'd met one of them a few days before, when he had translated for us from Inuktitut to English with great skill and humour. On this evening he conveyed embarrassment about how people inside the hall were eating. "These are very traditional people," he said. "We don't eat like that now, many of us. We're more modern today."

People inside the recreation centre had arrived from their homes with boxes of frozen char, salmon and caribou meat. Others had come with an abundance of cooked food, but we southerners were fascinated by delicacies like fermented walrus and seabirds (in some cases not only uncooked but also unplucked). Raw and frozen food was laid out on clean strips of cardboard in the centre of the hall floor, with the cooked food placed on tables at the front. The raw food diners knelt on the floor, showing the uninitiated how to cut a piece of frozen fish or fowl with a sharp knife and then chew vigorously. Visitors were told to "think sushi." Participants in the 2006 Ikkavak dogsled race had their eyes on the prizes awarded this night, everything from cash to expensive commodities not usually available here—stainless steel refrigerators and leather sofas. The prize Makivik is aiming for is something less tangible, and something it hopes will grow and endure: Inuk male pride. Today there are only 200 sled dogs remaining, but Makivik is breeding more, and only purebred Inuit husky dogs (not blue-eyed Siberian huskies) are permitted in the Ivakkak race.

Makivik held its annual general meeting in Kangirsuk during the 2006 Arctic tour, and it was wonderful to see a consensual government at work. Dozens of Inuit leaders (most of them male) were seated around tables in the school gymnasium, and simultaneous Inuktitut-to-English translation was provided for all the proceedings. I was delighted to find myself sitting alongside Harry Tulugak, the former mayor of Puvirnituq, who'd once taken a strong stand against the sale of alcohol and led his people out of a sexual abuse crisis through months of prayer and community meetings.

Kangirsuk appeared to be a peaceful, traditional Inuit community during my visit, but it faces the same problems other Nunavik communities are confronting. (Unknown to me then, there'd been two violent deaths in Kangirsuk just a month before our visit; both of the victims were women. Alcohol use in the community had been high the weekend the violence occurred.)

As I waited at the Kuujjuaq airport for my flight back to Montreal, I saw two young men swing a large unmarked cardboard box into a pickup truck parked in front of the Air Inuit hangar.

"We'll have to drink quick," one of them joked, "before it gets stolen." The contents of the box, flown in from a Montreal *dépanneur* (convenience store) 1,500 kilometres away, had been hard to come by: four cases of beer and a large bottle of Johnnie Walker. No retail sales of alcohol are allowed in Kangirsuk, Kuujjuaq or any other Inuit community in Nunavik, so the only way to get it for home consumption is to order it from one of several Montreal stores licensed to supply it. These men had paid $259 for forty-eight beers and a forty-ounce bottle of whiskey, plus $103 for air freight.

West of Kuujjuaq, in Iqaluit, Nunavut, residents have to apply for a permit to get alcohol, which is brought in by air from Rankin Inlet, 1,300 kilometres away. If you want to drink in Rankin Inlet, the alcohol has to be flown in from Iqaluit. Alcohol is flying around in planes across the North because the Inuit feel uneasy about making it too accessible on the ground. At the centre of this apparent madness are communities besieged by alcohol, drugs and gambling, with no idea how to control these things. Some communities have given up trying.

The RCMP head of Aboriginal policing says there are limits to what the police can do. "Technically, we don't have the authority to search luggage for alcohol, because it's not an illegal product," RCMP Director General Doug Reti told me. "We have to have grounds to conduct such a search." Ban or no ban, Reti said, where there's a thirst for alcohol a way will be found to get it. He has confiscated gas cans full of whiskey and old video recorders with flasks hidden inside. He believes tackling the causes of addiction would be more effective than stepping up enforcement.

Kuujjuaq is currently revisiting its ban on retail alcohol sales, to take business away not from bootleggers but from the Montreal *dépanneurs*. "Some of the benefits from these alcohol sales should come locally," said Kuujjuaq's thirty-eight-year-old mayor, Larry Watt. Watt has invited Kuujjuaq's non-profit organizations to compete for a permit to sell alcohol. The successful applicant will be required to invest the money earned back into the town, as the community's only bar does now; sales of alcohol there go to recreational programs.

A group of residents in Kuujjuaq, however, are concerned their efforts to reopen the town's only addiction treatment centre will be wasted if alcohol becomes more readily available.

The centre was closed because its programs were considered ineffective, and Jacob Partridge, an Inuit elder, was hired to make the treatment centre more culturally and spiritually suitable for Inuit. His original vision was to build a new centre on the edge of town that contained three buildings representing three different Inuit housing types, each with a different service, including relapse prevention. Lack of funding, though, means he will have to make do with the current sixty-year-old building, so small it can only treat nine addicts at a time.

David Forrest, the volunteer chair of the new treatment centre, remained optimistic that, even in its modest form, the centre will have an impact. "We are going to put the Inuit way of doing things into the treatment centre," he told me, "and adapt existing protocols to Inuit philosophy. I'm very excited about it. It's pretty neat."

Jacob Partridge worried about the mixed message to residents when the town's leadership was prepared to put profit before prevention. "Even though it would look like a good idea to get all these millions of dollars into the community," Partridge concluded, "who's going to get the addicts healed, who's going to get them out of it? For me, alcohol in any form is a deterrent for our people to go forward. The bar should be closed as well."

Forrest, a non-Aboriginal businessman in Kuujjuaq, used to binge drink with Inuit friends he had made over his thirty years of living there. Since becoming sober, he sees the community in a new light. "Sometimes when I land here in the plane, I can feel the pain of the people," he said. "We're faced with it every day, through the suicides, through the senseless violence that occurs and through the lack of hope we see in peoples' eyes."

Despite the initiatives being taken to curb the violence and addiction in Inuit communities, more concerted action is needed. Some leaders seem to hope the problem will diminish with time. A lot of damage will be done while they're waiting.

In the fall of 2007, the Inuit of Nunavut decided to organize their own inquiry into the killing of their sled dogs in the 1950s and '60s. They hired a retired Newfoundland and Labrador provincial court judge, James Igloliorte, an Inuk from Nunatsiavut, to run what they call a truth commission, using $600,000 provided by Tunngavik Inc., the organization that administers the Nunavut land claim. Makivik continues to push for a full federal government inquiry and awaits Igloliorte's findings with great interest.

The Power of Political Will
in the Northwest Territories

A SMALL BOY MOVING HOUSE FOR HIS DRUNKEN PARENTS inspired Dr. Jennifer Chalmers to write a forceful indictment of addiction services in the Northwest Territories.

"I was out for a drive in Fort McPherson and saw this five-year-old child," she recalled, "pulling a sled along a muddy path with two TVs, boxes, towels, some toys on it. When I offered to help he said, 'I'm moving. We were kicked out of our house because my parents are drinking.' There was no sign of his parents."

Chalmers is the lead author of "A State of Emergency: A Report on the Delivery of Addiction Services in the NWT." The report was first published in 2002, then updated in 2006 with a progress report on what the government has done. I visited Chalmers at her home in Regina, where she works as a consultant. She has received the ultimate compliment for her report: instead of shelving it, the Northwest Territories government is using it to set government policy. Members of the legislature frequently refer to the "Chalmers report" when they rise to speak about drug or alcohol abuse problems.

There are twice as many problem drinkers in the NWT as there are anywhere else in Canada. According to the latest (2006) Northwest Territories Addiction Survey, 31.2 per cent of the population fifteen years and older are classified as heavy drinkers, compared to 18 per cent in the Yukon, 15.4 per cent in Alberta and 12.7 per cent for all the provinces combined. More than half of the NWT's population has been harmed by someone's drinking. And Chalmers says that's not all.

"The greatest problem facing the people of the Northwest Territories," Chalmers writes in her report, "is addiction to substances such as alcohol, nicotine, marijuana and problem gambling... Improved economic opportunities as the result of oil, gas and mineral exploration have done little to decrease the incidence of addictions."

On weekends, she told me, some NWT communities are eerily quiet during the day. "Where are the children? They're not outside, because they are still sleeping during the day. Their parents haven't gotten up yet. Perhaps they've been attending an all-night bingo game. Gambling is becoming fast and furious a more debilitating addiction. The women are leaving the alcohol and moving to the gambling. And as far as the devastation to the family, not only is there the physical part of the alcohol or the smoking or the drugs, now there is gambling on top of that. When the parents are absent, children are left raising themselves."

In addition, according to the 1996 Northwest Territories Alcohol and Drug survey, 11 per cent of people in the NWT have tried using solvents to get high and the rate is as high today. Chalmers was shocked to discover that, despite all that was known about the need for addiction services in 2002, only 3 per cent of the Territories' Health and Social Services budget was spent on treatment and prevention.

"You can't go to a band council meeting, a school meeting, the RCMP, and not hear about the problems with the youth in terms of alcohol and drug use," she told me. "If you ask for support from any community agency for anything to do with addictions, mental health, substance abuse, everyone will sign up. You'll have ten people right away. So the overwhelming demand and the urgency have been there."

Chalmers successfully communicated that sense of urgency and closed the gap between policy and reality when she wrote "A State of Emergency." Addiction services, she said, had been drastically cut since she first began working in the NWT. The Gwich'in Tribal Council hired her eighteen years ago to set up a family treatment program aimed at motivating addicts to stop hurting their families and bring reconciliation between parents and children. She's maintained a close relationship with Gwich'in communities since then, helping to devise suicide prevention strategies, offering trauma and grief counselling, and even providing mental health services from a tent in remote hunting camps, an experience she enjoys. She has earned the trust of the Territories' Aboriginal population, approximately 20,000 people in thirty-two communities spread out over an area the size of India. There are an equal number of non-Aboriginals in the Northwest Territories, mostly living in the capital, Yellowknife.

Chalmers has four university degrees in psychology, and she completed her Doctorate at the prestigious Adler School of Psychology in Chicago. She's done post-graduate training in substance abuse, group therapy and child psychology. She's also a warm, personable woman of Mohawk and Micmac ancestry with a passion for her work, because alcoholism has been a problem in her extended family. The drastic cuts her report documents came after the NWT government decided to close three of its four residential treatment centres in the mid-1990s, as emphasis throughout North America shifted from treating addicts at residential centres to relying on outpatient clinics. Unfortunately, the government didn't reinvest what it saved by closing these centres. Instead, spending on addiction services went from $14 to $15 million in 1994–95 to just $3 million by 2001. The slow deterioration caused by the cuts had rendered the system useless by the time Chalmers conducted her evaluation.

"The whole system of addiction services lacks credibility from the client's perspective, the government perspective, from the health care sector, and from the community perspective," her report states.

What happened in the NWT should serve as a cautionary tale for governments elsewhere in Canada. Effective professional services must be made available at the same time the causes of addiction are addressed. Like the false fronts in TV westerns, Chalmers and her colleagues found that community services in the NWT had become shells; they gave the appearance that something was being done when really nothing was. Community addiction programs were underfunded, housed in poor facilities, and staffed by demoralized people, 37 per cent of whom had no education or qualifications related to their jobs. There was "an overall lack of expertise, knowledge and skill of the personnel involved in the delivery of addictions services," Chalmers wrote. Nurses knew little or nothing about addictions, yet they were the ones expected to cope with the fallout from a drunken spree or drug overdose. "Nursing staff are overworked and often understaffed," the initial report says. "They are also very frustrated with the lack of qualified staff in addictions."

What was happening was a huge disservice, Chalmers' report concluded, to the Aboriginal population most in need of social healing: "In recent years, there has been an increasing recognition of the effects of trauma, physical and sexual abuse from residential school experiences and family violence as major determinants in the progression of addictions in residents of the NWT. Many Aboriginal groups are now referring to healing as a more holistic way of dealing with addictions and their consequences...It is unfortunate to report such disappointing news regarding the total inadequacy of the Community Addictions Services in the NWT. Good quality addictions services are not a luxury for NWT residents but a requirement for health, well-being and self-sufficiency."

When Chalmers' "State of Emergency" report came out, there was widespread acceptance of its findings. No one defended the system that was in place. In 2002, the newly appointed minister of health and social services for the NWT, Michael Miltenberger (he became deputy premier in 2007), agreed to tear down the feeble foundation of his department's addiction programming and rebuild it from scratch. From the increased budget his department was given, he allocated $7 million a year for addiction and mental health services, which are combined in the Northwest Territories.

"We laid out a comprehensive plan to restructure the entire social services and health care system," he told me during an interview by phone in May 2006, "and made addictions and mental health a core service." The plan also looks to the future, Miltenberger said. "Our health indicators tell us alcohol consumption is two times the national average, smoking, family violence, sexually transmitted infections . . . they're all linked together. So a major development like the Mackenzie Valley pipeline, if we're not properly prepared, will exacerbate the already bad indicators."

Miltenberger followed Chalmers' guidelines and the forty-eight recommendations in her report almost to the letter. Seventy-seven new jobs were created for workers in the mental health and addictions sphere. In 2006, there were twenty graduates from a program called "community wellness"; workers in that field run alcohol, drug abuse and suicide prevention programs. They are called out when there's a suicide to help coordinate the community's response, in particular to help prevent the cluster of suicides that often follow. Twenty-five new nurses finished their training at Aurora College in Yellowknife in 2006, bringing Chalmers' dream of a "northern health workforce" closer to reality. In July 2007, the Northwest Territories signed a memorandum of agreement with the Canadian Centre on Substance Abuse to continue developing the territories' skill level in the field of addictions treatment and prevention.

"We've also instituted a nurse practitioner program, and have graduates coming out there as well. We'll bring them into the communities as fast as we can train them," Michael Miltenberger told me. "We've added a midwifery program, made midwifery an insured service and we're getting that out into the communities."

All of this has been accomplished in a very short time.

"The rebuilding has begun," Chalmers writes in her 2006 progress report called "Stay the Course . . . and Together

We Can Secure the Foundation That Has Been Built." She describes a social system that has been wakened from sleep and is now dynamic, changing to accommodate the recommendations she made in 2002. But her progress report warns against complacency.

"The current funding of community-based services is a huge step in the right direction," she writes in "Stay the Course," "and ongoing investments are needed to further develop and solidify these investments in the mental health and addiction core service." The seventy-seven new workers, for example, are being paid half what their counterparts receive in the rest of Canada. And those counterparts themselves receive less than their work is worth, according to Chalmers. "The work is very undervalued, extremely undervalued, so people don't stay in it," she told me. "In fact, much bias [regarding people's pay and qualifications] was heard with respect to how job descriptions are reviewed."

Chalmers' progress report offers a number of recommendations about how the Territories can build on the work that has been done. Most of all, she wants government to seize the moment, to build on the goodwill she found. "The passion and devotion to addressing the mental health, addiction, and family violence problems is limitless right across the NWT," she notes in "Stay the Course." "People and groups at the community level realize there are no quick fix solutions, no miracle programs and few complete answers in dealing with the magnitude and complexity of addiction and mental health problems."

IT'S CLEAR FROM reading the Hansard of the Northwest Territories legislature that alcohol abuse and the problems that come with it are huge public policy issues in this part of Canada. Fresh food runs out in the North. Fresh milk and vegetables can be hard to come by. There's always lot's of booze, though, and it's supplied by the government. Michael Miltenberger believes it's a moral imperative to control alcohol availability. But when he was the NWT's minister of health, Miltenberger's hands were tied. In the Northwest Territories, the minister of finance has the responsibility for selling alcohol.

"If I had one wish," the health minister told me, "I would wish that we had no more alcohol in communities, and I tell people that within eight hours, in one day, you'd see things improving, guaranteed. The shelters would start emptying out, the jails would start releasing people who'd be back in school, working, and FASD babies would stop—the whole quality of life would so improve."

In January 2006, the Northwest Territories updated legislation regarding its Liquor Licensing Agency and, in doing so, it disregarded public opinion. "Improving Liquor Legislation in the NWT—Final Report of the 2005 Liquor Act Review" was released by Floyd Roland, then minister of finance. At public hearings held in advance of the report, people in the NWT had asked that a percentage of liquor sales be allocated for prevention and addiction programs. Yet the government concluded: "Earmarking is the only issue raised during the Liquor Act Review that was strongly supported by the public, yet completely unsupported by best practices or background documentation." For that reason, profits from selling alcohol in the Northwest Territories will stay in the treasury. Communities that requested "special prohibition orders"—times when alcohol would not be sold—were also turned down. "Businesses incur high costs when they are forced to close during a prohibition period," the legislators argued. The only time the Liquor Licensing Agency might allow prohibition, the report said, is during a serious community situation, such as a public health crisis or a time of heightened violence. There was no indication of how high violence levels would have to climb before a particular community's request would be considered.

In the winter of 2006 the Ministry of Health and Social Services launched a major public relations campaign against smoking.

"Why not instigate public education campaigns on the same scale to discourage alcohol abuse?" I asked Miltenberger, during our interview.

"How do you encourage people to drink responsibly?" he said. "Or tell people to go for total abstinence?"

"Some clever advertisers could come up with a campaign," I suggested.

"Attitudes have turned around substantially for tobacco," he replied, "but I don't think they could for alcohol. It's easier to single tobacco out as a villain. Alcohol exists in many forms, and you don't have the issue of second-hand smoke."

There are the second-hand effects of alcohol abuse on children, I suggested.

"You can drink responsibly and enjoy it," he told me. "My dad used to enjoy a cold beer after working out in the garden, and it can be done. Look at what the big beer and liquor companies spend on liquor advertising. We're just bombarded with 'If you want a good time, you've got to have a fridge full of beer, and good things will happen.' "

"Isn't the situation urgent enough to make the beer companies more responsible?" I asked.

"That's part of the challenge," Miltenberger admitted. "But it always comes back to how peoples' health is a personal choice and a personal responsibility. You have to convince people to make the right choices. That's the fundamental challenge for us. Otherwise, we'll never have enough money to build all the hospitals and all the treatment centres and all the facilities needed to help them once they're in crisis. If you don't focus on the front end, to get people to make the right choices, it's unsustainable to continue on. There'll never be enough doctors, nurses and social workers."

ABORIGINAL COMMUNITIES IN the Northwest Territories turned to Jennifer Chalmers for help once again in the summer of 2006, this time in dealing with almost overwhelming grief. There had been two suicides in Fort McPherson, and a terrible plane crash had killed five people from Fort Good Hope. Chalmers flew in to listen and offer advice. The communities knew there was a risk these incidents might set back the progress they had made in stemming the tide of addiction and social despair. Like Chalmers herself, they were determined to build on their successes and keep moving forward.

Health Canada:

Addicted to Control

WHEN CAMILLE FOUILLARD UNPLUGGED THE COFFEE urn after a long day of meetings and carried it to her car, she inadvertently created a mess for an Aboriginal man trying to work within Canada's bureaucratic culture.

Jack Penashue groaned when he saw the stream of coffee grounds that had leaked from the urn, staining the carpet at Health Canada's boardroom in Sheshatshiu. Fouillard, a non-Aboriginal health consultant, is based in Halifax. Penashue, an Innu social worker in Sheshatshiu, spent the next forty-five minutes scrubbing out the stains. He didn't want to fulfill a bureaucrat's prediction that he was not responsible enough to use the room properly.

"It doesn't matter that you did this," Penashue told Fouillard, to explain why he was cleaning so diligently. "It'll be blamed on me because I'm Innu."

Many Canadians would balk at the suggestion that our institutions are racist, but the creation-process of one of

Canada's most comprehensive public health campaigns against Aboriginal addictions is a case in point.

Jack Penashue, a recovered alcoholic, fought tremendous personal odds to earn a degree in social work from the University of Regina. Scrubbing out coffee grounds is just one of a number of humbling tasks he's willing to do if they will bring back the good mental and physical health that his people enjoyed sixty years ago. At the time of the coffee grounds spill, Penashue worked on contract for Health Canada. (Today he provides child protection services in his home community.) He had expected support for the weekend meeting he'd organized and was surprised when he was refused the key to the Health Canada boardroom at first. The key was released only after a stern warning that there be no damage.

"Would they even bring up the issue of damage with another social worker?" Penashue asked Fouillard. "I don't think so. Where's the trust?"

The trust takes a long time to establish, according to Sarah Archer, at the time the Health Canada director responsible for the Labrador Innu Comprehensive Healing Strategy. In the spring of 2006, she spoke to me by telephone from her office in Halifax. I pressed Archer to describe what concrete action had occurred since the healing plan was implemented. "We have people in place to provide professional support [to the Innu communities]," she told me. "And we're working much more closely with them [the Innu] than ever before, but it goes back to the process of relationship building. It takes much longer with Aboriginal communities than it does with other communities. That's been my experience over twenty-something years. You need to build that trust and rapport."

(If what Archer said is true, what can Health Canada expect to achieve with a ten-year healing plan? Much time has already been lost because of the uneasy relationship that existed for so long between the bureaucrats and the people they were paid to serve. The players on the Innu side have not changed since the healing plan was established, but Archer has since left Health Canada, and the department has brought several new people to the process.)

The Labrador Innu Comprehensive Healing Strategy is Canada's most ambitious effort to reduce addiction levels in Aboriginal communities. This effort, focussed on Labrador, has been ongoing for seven years, and an evaluation of its progress suggests that Health Canada's strategy for the region needs serious surgery.

The shocking images broadcast in 2000 of Innu children in Sheshatshiu and Davis Inlet inhaling solvents, and the intense publicity that followed, weren't enough to push the federal government into high gear. It took a plea made by a delegation from Davis Inlet to the Shawinigan home of Jean Chretien, prime minister at the time, to finally tip the scales in the Innu's favour. At the prime minister's insistence, the ministers of Health and Indian and Northern Affairs convened a high-level meeting with Treasury Board and Solicitor General officials to commit money for a new strategy they agreed to make top priority. Health Canada took responsibility for advancing community health issues; Indian Affairs agreed to relocate the people of Davis Inlet to Natuashish and to fast-track reserve status for the Labrador Innu; the Solicitor General's office committed to improving community policing. The Labrador Innu Comprehensive Healing Strategy received Cabinet approval in June 2001, but there was an extraordinary oversight: the Innu were left out of the planning process. Sarah Archer agreed in 2006 that this was a big mistake.

"After an initial hiccup," she told me, "we learned that we had to work with the Innu in all stages—priority setting and planning, program development and implementation."

Hiccup seems a mild word for not involving the Innu in their own healing plan from the outset. Today, the bureaucratic sense of urgency has lost momentum, and it is being outpaced by the rate at which young Innu are turning to alcohol and drugs to deal with their emotional pain and with lives of stifling boredom.

"The youth who were inhaling solvents are doing drugs now," says Kathleen Benuen, Natuashish's health director.

In 2001, $59 million was committed by Indian and Northern Affairs Canada to build the new community of Natuashish; $20 million was allocated for Health Canada programs in Labrador, and $2 million for the Solicitor General's community policing work. In 2004, INAC received another $15 million and Health Canada, $5 million. In 2005, $102 million more was allocated to keep the strategy in place until 2010. Surely ten years and $203 million should be enough to "cure" 3,000 Aboriginal people of addictions that became part of their culture only in the 1960s. But with just two years left in its mandate, its priorities must shift if the Labrador Innu Comprehensive Healing Strategy is to have any impact at all. The biggest stumbling block to progress, according to the Innu, is the Labrador Health Secretariat, the bureaucracy set up to administer the healing plan.

A taxi driver was stumped when I asked him to take me to the secretariat's offices in Goose Bay in 2005. It's hard to keep secrets in this town of 7,000, but the location of Health Canada's base of operations in Labrador is obviously one of them. After some consultation with the dispatcher, the driver left me at the back of a building in an industrial part of town. The entrance door was locked, but there was an intercom. I found the secretariat's offices at the top of a steep narrow staircase.

Amazingly, the secretariat was initially based in Halifax, thousands of kilometres from the people it was meant to serve. Pressure from the Innu forced its relocation to Goose Bay, eastern Labrador's biggest town, but that did little to affect the secretariat's perceived remoteness from its clients. After more pressure, six of the twenty-one jobs created at the secretariat were moved into the two communities that are the focus of its work—Sheshatshiu and Natuashish.

In 2003, a team of health researchers from Memorial University's School of Medicine conducted an evaluation of the Labrador Innu Comprehensive Healing Strategy. Their report, "Beginning the Journey to Change," provides insight into how much time was wasted because of the gulf between the bureaucrats and the Innu. The report depicts a strategy top-heavy with administrators but light on the skilled people needed to conduct addiction therapy, counselling and mental health support: skills the Innu had requested training for. The report found that the strategy also lacked clear and decisive direction.

"Healing strategy programs in Sheshatshiu and Natuashish do not appear to follow any specific intervention model," the report's authors wrote. The report recommended the adoption of known community addiction strategies, but to date that recommendation has still not been followed.

One well-known model recommend by the Memorial University report is the "Community Readiness Model," pioneered at Colorado State University. A Cherokee woman named Pamela Jumper-Thurman co-developed the model after years of frontline work in Aboriginal communities in the United

States. Jumper-Thurman's process begins with an assessment of the psychological readiness of a community in distress to undergo change. There's no point in providing services, Jumper-Thurman believes, if public education and community awareness building haven't first created an enthusiastic client base for the programs to be offered. Next there must be seeds planted for community development.

Communities, like individuals, can be in denial about their problems, but Jumper-Thurman believes community-wide change can be made if just a few people, acting as catalysts, begin the process by taking the steps her model outlines. "Community members become involved in identifying and owning the problem," she writes in a paper published in 2000, "just as family members identify the problems in therapy. They identify potential barriers in their own language and context, and collaborate in the development of interventions (similar to a family treatment plan) that are culturally consistent with their populations."

I asked Health Canada's Sarah Archer why the secretariat in Goose Bay was not acting on the Memorial University evaluators' recommendation to use such a model.

"Partly because we don't actually do program delivery," she said. "We support the community in their own program delivery." When I asked what the fifteen people in the Goose Bay office actually do, Archer told me, "They provide professional expertise. There are nurses to guide on maternal health issues, a nutritionist, a specialist on early childhood development and someone who works with the family on health care for support workers."

An incident I witnessed in December 2005 had already raised questions for me about how engaged in the healing process the Goose Bay bureaucrats were. I was visiting in Sheshatshiu when Tshaukuesh got a phone call from a friend in Labrador City, telling her about an important meeting in Goose Bay he thought she should attend. He explained that the government of Newfoundland and Labrador was holding the last of its public hearings on revisions to the *Mental Health and Addictions Act*. I accompanied Tshaukuesh, her son Jack, Edward Nuna and Jack's wife, Rena, to the Goose Bay hotel where the meeting was taking place. They were the only Aboriginals in attendance. Jack suggested to the group that the province's legislation be updated to include the protection of children who abuse solvents, a problem that didn't exist when the legislation was first drafted in the 1950s. The meeting facilitator, after commenting that this was the first time the issue had been raised, wrote Jack's suggestion on a flip chart. No one from the Health Secretariat had signalled this important issue or attended the hearings. Later, Jack told me about another meeting he had attended in Goose Bay; a bevy of government representatives had flown in from Ottawa and Nova Scotia to discuss the requirements for women's shelters in Sheshatshiu and Natuashish. As the visitors chattered on, Jack told me, they seemed unconscious of his presence and that of a woman from his community, the only other Innu person present. Jack leaned towards his Innu companion at one point and whispered, "Is it just me, or do you feel left out of our healing plan, too?"

A HEALTH SECRETARIAT memo, written in June 2006, made Nympha Byrne feel left out of the process, and at times, deeply offended by it. The word "Draft" was stamped in the upper left-hand corner, below the Labrador Health Secretariat's letterhead. The words "Safety and Security: Travelling to Nat-uashish" were printed in bold. Knowing her colleagues were reading the memo too made the forty-six-year-old Innu woman sad and ashamed.

"The well being of staff is of utmost importance when trav-elling," the memo read. "It is preferred that staff travel in pairs when going to Natuashish."

The people Byrne loves most in the world live in Natuash-ish, her birthplace. As the secretariat's only full-time Innu employee, she was humiliated and insulted by the memo's implication that her people were somehow dangerous.

"I couldn't face the staff meeting," she told me. "I just went home."

Byrne couldn't understand why the warning was neces-sary, since no Health Canada employee has ever been hurt in Natuashish.

"I don't think that's fair to our people," she said.

The memo offended the leader of another Innu commu-nity, too.

"Why are Health Canada staff talking about their own safety when we have children who are not safe in our commu-nities?" asked Anastasia Qupee, the chief of Sheshatshiu. "We still have children walking around late at night. There are lots of drugs in the communities, a lot of children in temporary care. They're supposed to be helping us. What are they doing? That memo may have ended our only hope of being able to work together."

I told this story to Dr. Valerie Gideon, while she was senior director of health and social policy at the Assembly of First Nations. We spoke at the group's annual general assembly in Vancouver in 2006. Gideon wasn't surprised. Civil servants are not the best people to implement healing strategies, she said, because they answer to politicians and senior bureaucrats, not to people in communities. There are other structural problems within Health Canada, she pointed out.

"The First Nations and Inuit Health Branch is not fully recognized as a health system within the Canadian health care system," Gideon said, "so it is subject to the rules and procedures that all federal departments are subject to. It means you have a lot of paperwork, you have checks and balances and a lot of procedures that are not appropriate for a health system."

(These days, Gideon is trying to change the system from within. In October 2007, she became Ontario's regional director of Health Canada's First Nations and Inuit Health Branch.)

The civil servants involved in the Labrador Innu Comprehensive Healing Strategy are in uncharted waters, Gideon told me, doing a job for which they have not received specialized training. The strategy is supposed to rebuild a society whose traditional economy and culture have been almost destroyed.

Sharon Clarke was also not surprised to hear that Health Canada's Goose Bay employees were afraid to go to Natuashish alone. Before becoming executive director of the National Native Addictions Partnership Foundation (NNAPF) in 2000, Clarke had worked for Health Canada's NNADAP program in Saskatchewan.

"I noticed in the nineties that a lot of Health Canada employees were afraid to go to reserves," she told me. "There was nothing to be afraid of. I always wondered where they got some of those ideas from."

NNAPF is creating a cross-cultural course that will be available for bureaucrats and others working in Aboriginal communities. Clarke told me she hoped the training will make people less fearful of their clients by teaching them about language, traditions and the historical context of social problems. "Anybody who wants to work in Aboriginal communities will have to have that module before they go in," she told me.

Nympha Byrne received an apology from her boss for the insensitive memo, but she still finds it very hard to do her job. Byrne is trained as an addiction therapist, but because of the secretariat's mandate, she spends most of her time at the Goose Bay office. "Sometimes I'm ashamed to say that I'm a Health Canada worker," Byrne told me in December 2005 while I was in Natuashish. She keeps a house there and an apartment in Goose Bay. "When I'm in Natuashish, I see kids on the road sniffing gas, and I'm not allowed to counsel them. I'm only allowed to do presentations. I find that really painful."

As a former binge drinker herself, Byrne brings her own experience into the equation. She thinks she'd be more helpful working in Natuashish, where she knows the people and speaks the language. Even though she's the only secretariat employee with this knowledge, her requests to set up a small satellite office of the secretariat in her home community have been turned down. "I don't think they trust me to work out of their sight," she told me.

As Sarah Archer says, the job of secretariat staff is to provide advice and to help manage the money that is being spent. The secretariat supports communities in their own program delivery, she told me. But that's only as long as these are programs approved by the bureaucrats. The Innu have some control over smaller budgets. The health commissions in the two main communities have budgets of approximately $1 million a year to pay for addiction and mental health services, including salaries, along with early childhood development, maternal nutrition and diabetes prevention programs.

Sheshatshiu's health director, Mary May Osmonde, told me she was very impressed by the work an Innu-speaking therapist from Quebec was offering communities there, but she could not get support from Health Canada to involve the woman in the Labrador healing plan.

The health commissions in Sheshatshiu and Natuashish are centres of hope in their communities. But Innu workers lack training and feel inadequate to fully address people's complex health and social needs. Osmonde has had no specific training for the job she holds now, or for the job she did previously, as community health planner.

Memorial University's "Beginning the Journey to Change" report identified training for Innu people as an urgent need. "With so much required of the Innu in terms of how programs and services will be delivered in the communities," the report said, "local capacity will be very important." Four years after the report was released, however, only an assessment of Innu training needs has been achieved. At this rate, the Innu fear the healing strategy's ten-year mandate will be complete before anyone is fully trained. As outlined earlier, over the same period of time in the Northwest Territories, a great deal has been accomplished, thanks to the development of specialized courses delivered by a college in Yellowknife and the political will to do something about the problem.

"The health secretariat is supposed to be providing expertise," Mary May Osmonde told me. "But we rarely see them in our communities. We don't know what they are doing in their offices. I'm very disappointed. Maybe the government wants us to fail. If we succeed and our people are healed, many bureaucrats will lose their jobs."

Osmonde's suggestion that civil servants profit from Aboriginal suffering may not be simply rhetorical. Valerie

Gideon says the needs of Aboriginal communities are routinely traded off to preserve jobs ("full-time equivalents") within the civil service. For example, instead of putting the $5 million it had surplus to its 2006 budget into Aboriginal communities, the First Nations and Inuit Health Branch shored up civil servant jobs at its regional and Ottawa offices.

"The priority will be to preserve the federal human resources and infrastructure and not the community infrastructure," Gideon told me. The same thing is happening with Health Canada's funding to protect Aboriginal people from the effects of an influenza pandemic, she said. "Any additional resources that FNIHB has received have gone towards setting up a major office of community medicine that has forty full-time equivalents. They are really investing in their own capacity. They have not replicated that investment in First Nations communities or in First Nations organizations."

Evaluators of the Innu healing plan write that the success or failure of the strategy will be answered by this question: "Are Labrador Innu children still dying? Success will occur if the children live in a safe community surrounded by healthy people, with less exposure to, or experience with, substance abuse. In short, the success of the strategy relates to whether or not the children have a positive future." The Innu think the Labrador Health Secretariat should be disbanded, with the money it receives given to their communities so they can heal themselves. The Innu nation has formally asked the Newfoundland and Labrador government to raise the issue with its federal counterparts. Provincial Aboriginal Affairs Minister Tom Rideout did so in February 2005 to no avail.

The health secretariat has a new director who is working closely with the Innu, and things are looking up. But a lot of time has been wasted, and the Healing Strategy's funds will run out in 2010.

"Health Canada needs to review what its role is," Sharon Clarke told me. "Currently it slows things down—withholding money, trying to control things. It's not the accountability that kills us, it's the control. You hire people who are supposed to provide advice to you, and they're afraid to go into your communities? It's ridiculous. And so are those big gates and pass codes at their buildings. I think it's totally disrespectful and stupid."

17

Affirmative Action
in British Columbia

THE RELIEF AND JUBILATION THAT FOLLOWED THE SIGN-
ing of the Kelowna Accord in November 2005 was short-lived.
Prior to the federal election that followed a few months later,
the Conservative Finance critic, Monte Solberg, had told a
Saskatchewan radio station that the accord was "something
the Liberals crafted at the last minute on the back of a napkin."
That's how easily the Conservative government led by Stephen
Harper dismissed the accord when they came to power, despite
the fact it was a negotiated deal between Aboriginal leaders, the
federal government, the territories and the provinces. When
I spoke to Jim Prentice, Harper's first minister of Indian and
Northern Affairs, in the fall of 2006, Prentice insisted that his
presence at a meeting of First Nations chiefs in Manitoba was
more significant to Aboriginal people than the accord had been:
"What I'm telling you is that no one raised the issue of Kelowna

with me in a four and a half hour meeting with seventy chiefs in Manitoba," he said by telephone from a Calgary hotel room, where he was preparing to attend a banquet. "All of those chiefs were happy to have a chance to meet the minister of Indian and northern affairs for the first time in twelve years."

Prentice was either terribly out of step with the Aboriginal mood or bluffing. The Kelowna Accord meant a lot to Aboriginal people in this country. Its creation was seen as an act of reconciliation, its demise as another knife in a very deep wound.

In an article in the November 2007 issue of *Walrus* magazine, Inuit leader Mary Simon is emphatic about what has been lost, particularly for people in the North. "Key among these [programs promised by the accord] was substantive funding for housing, where overcrowding and hidden homelessness are rampant," she writes. "Kelowna promised 1,200 housing units over five years. These vanished when the Liberal government fell. The current government did earmark $200 million for new housing in Nunavut, but it has not provided the needed funding in other regions where Inuit are located. Similarly, $1.3 billion for Aboriginal health care and $1.8 billion for education have not been provided."

Groundwork for the Kelowna Accord had been laid many months before the Conservatives came to power. In October 2005, I attended a news conference in St. John's in which B.C. Premier Gordon Campbell added Danny Williams, premier of Newfoundland and Labrador, to his list of Canadian leaders supporting the proposed agreement. Williams' cooperation in the initiative made support for the agreement unanimous among territorial leaders and provincial premiers. Almost a year later, I met Campbell when he came to St. John's for the annual premiers' conference in July 2006. I was curious to know how he was taking the failure of the accord he had helped to draft. When we met at his hotel, I noticed he was carrying a copy of James Frey's memoir, *A Million Little Pieces*.

He was determined to keep Aboriginal needs on the national political agenda, Campbell told me. Just days before, he'd held a mini summit with the premiers and Assembly of First Nations National Chief Phil Fontaine. Campbell had wrung commitments from three of the premiers to host events that would advance Aboriginal policy, he said. For example, the Newfoundland government had promised to hold a national Aboriginal women's summit, which it did in the spring of 2007. If he felt displeasure with Prime Minister Harper for killing the Kelowna Accord, Campbell didn't show it in public. He simply reiterated his personal commitment to the new policy direction he had forged with B.C.'s Aboriginals in March 2005. "The New Relationship with Aboriginal People" is a policy statement that commits the province of British Columbia to substantive changes in the way it deals with First Nations and Metis people. (There are no Inuit in British Columbia.) "We agree to a new government-to-government relationship based on respect, recognition and accommodation of Aboriginal title and rights," the statement reads. The government department responsible is called the Ministry of Aboriginal Relations and Reconciliation.

Campbell spoke enthusiastically to me about his policy's objectives. "The *Indian Act* needs major renovation. Land rights have to be resolved. There's a lot to be considered," he said. "But I'm not the one making the changes. The Aboriginal leadership is going to do that. They're driving this new relationship."

When British Columbia came into Confederation in 1871, it brought with it cultures Canadians are proud to display in museums and art galleries. The creators of those masks and totem poles, however, were offered few treaties, and they were effectively cut out of the country's public life through laws that barred them from voting (Aboriginal people couldn't vote in federal elections until 1960) or from raising money to pursue land claims.

Today, there are 198 First Nations with Aboriginal title in British Columbia. The courts say the title issue must be dealt with before provincial economic development can continue at its former pace. That's one good reason for the B.C. government to forge a new relationship with First Nations. Aboriginal people are divided on whether Campbell's motivation is based primarily on moral or on practical considerations. They have to admit, though, that he's putting money where his mouth is. Campbell's government has set aside $100 million to help First Nations prepare for land claim and self-government negotiations. No other provincial government has been as generous. The *New Relationship Trust Act,* in effect March 31, 2006, lays out how the trust funds are to be spent over the next ten years. Campbell has a lofty goal, he told me; he wants the First Nations and Metis standard of living in British Columbia raised to the provincial average by 2016. There's a lot of work ahead considering that First Nations residents in the province have one of the lowest standards of living in the country.

Campbell is prepared to go it alone, but he would rather have Ottawa's support. If that means swallowing the loss of the Kelowna Accord without rancour, he seems prepared to do it. Later that month, I would watch him work with Indian and Northern Affairs minister Jim Prentice at a news conference held at the Xweme'lch'stn Estimxwawtxw school in North Vancouver. There, both levels of government ceremoniously handed over control of Aboriginal education to the communities that are part of B.C.'s First Nations Education Steering Committee. Right now just half of B.C.'s Aboriginal students graduate from high school. The picture is not much better across the country, and other provinces would do well to follow the B.C. example.

As our interview in St. John's drew to an end, I asked Campbell why he was reading Frey's memoir about a life rebuilt after addiction. He told me his father had been an alcoholic and a physician who committed suicide when Campbell was just thirteen.

"The book talks about the self-loathing of the addict," Campbell said. "Addiction is no different for Aboriginal people than it is for us. It's self-medication. We've been putting First Nations down for years and years. We have to start recognizing their strengths, their languages and cultural diversity, to reinforce their pride."

Campbell's staunch support for Aboriginal rights, his comfort in using the word "nations," characterize what one critic would call "Aboriginal orthodoxy."

Tom Flanagan, a professor at the University of Calgary and the political advisor who directed Stephen Harper's election campaign, opposes what he sees as the uncritical acceptance of Aboriginal rights in Canadian public policy. "The Aboriginal orthodoxy encourages Aboriginal people to withdraw into themselves . . . under their own self-governments, on their own traditional lands, on their own Aboriginal economies," Flanagan writes in his book, *First Nations? Second Thoughts.*

Flanagan argues that prior residence in North America does not entitle Aboriginal people to special treatment and that separating them further from the mainstream will not bring them independence or prosperity. When I spoke with him, federal minister Jim Prentice denied that Flanagan's opinions were influencing his government's Aboriginal policy, but it's hard to imagine this is not the case. The Conservative government under Stephen Harper has not held a policy conference on Aboriginal affairs since its election, and the direction the Conservatives plan to take in this area is still something of a mystery.

"Prosperity and self-sufficiency require a willingness to integrate into the economy and move to where the jobs are," Flanagan writes. "Heavy subsidies for the reserve economies are producing two extremes—a well-to-do entrepreneurial and professional elite and an increasing number of welfare-dependent Indians."

Gordon Campbell holds a different view. "I'm not afraid of small governments," he told me, referring to the prospect of Aboriginal communities governing themselves and developing their own economies. "Rural development is a challenge across this country, but that doesn't mean we should abandon that challenge. Look at what's happening on the Osoyoos reserve in the Okanagan Valley. There's virtually no unemployment."

The Osoyoos First Nation owns a company called Inkameep Vineyards Limited, one of the largest vineyards in British Columbia. The band plans to capitalize on cultural tourism as well. It has partnered with a neighbouring ski resort to attract visitors coming to the province for the winter Olympics in 2010. "Clarence Louie has been their chief for twenty years," Campbell said, "and you can see that they look up to him."

Tom Flanagan thinks such Aboriginal leaders are an exception. "The problem is not that Indian leaders are especially

venal," he writes, "although many are . . . Chiefs and councillors have a greater opportunity to appoint their relatives and
supporters to jobs, to sign contracts with well-connected businesses and to manipulate the assignment of property rights. It
is a fertile field for factionalism."

Gordon Campbell, though, says the *Indian Act* foisted a
form of government on First Nations that is inferior to what
they had traditionally.

"Who decided they were going to have elected band coun-
cils?" Campbell asked during our conversation. "The hereditary
chiefs structure worked well for centuries. First Nations people had high regard for their elders. We can't hold First Nations
people responsible for decisions they didn't make."

Campbell envisions a province, he told me, where the
cultural diversity of First Nations is celebrated as part of the
provincial identity. The evolution of the premier's Aboriginal
policy is hard to track. He insists there was no epiphany. Yet
many feel Campbell's 2005 Speech from the Throne was an
abrupt about-face from the previous Liberal position. Some
have credited Jessica McDonald, his deputy minister in charge
of strategic planning, who was brought into government in the
fall of 2004 after many years of working with native bands
on land-use planning and environmental issues. Whatever
the source, there is an important tone of reconciliation in the
province's stated policy objectives.

"Your government regrets the tragic experiences visited
upon First Nations through years of paternalistic policies . . .
that fostered inequity, intolerance, isolation and indifference,"
Campbell's 2005 throne speech read. "Inadequate education,
health care and housing; rampant unemployment; alcoholism and drug abuse; unconscionably high rates of physical

and sexual abuse, incarceration, infant mortality and suicide: these are the hallmarks of despair that have disproportionately afflicted First Nations families, on and off-reserve ... Your government is determined to provide a new level of economic opportunity for First Nations communities and people."

In *First Nations? Second Thoughts*, Tom Flanagan argues that supporting Aboriginal self-determination will not help to end addiction and other social ills. Flanagan believes encouraging a myriad of small, "ethnically diverse" governments poses an unacceptable risk to Canadian sovereignty. "Perhaps the damage to Canada would be tolerable if it meant that Aboriginal peoples would escape from the social pathologies in which they are mired to become prosperous, self-supporting citizens," he writes, "but I believe the actual outcome ... would be quite different. Canada and Aboriginal peoples would become worse off than they should be."

Gordon Campbell, by contrast, asserts that it is in the national interest to listen to the solutions Aboriginal people propose for the problems they face. Overwhelmingly, Aboriginals say a return to their cultural and traditional roots is needed to restore social health.

"For me and for many Canadians," Campbell told me, "it's a moral and ethical issue. We have to recognize what happened. It's not acceptable to have a Third Solitude. If they're out of sight, they're out of mind."

The pace of resolving land claims is still slow in British Columbia, but it is moving faster there than anywhere else in the country. Campbell's advocacy is a bright spot on an otherwise bleak political horizon. The optimistic mood in Aboriginal communities across the country as 2005 came to a close has been replaced by one of deep concern. Gordon

Campbell shares that concern, he told me, and he seems determined to do something about it.

"We have two choices. We can continue to build a culture of dependency and a culture of addiction, of denial and despair, or we can make every effort to create a culture of hope, a culture of education and opportunity," Campbell said as our interview came to a close. "Let's build a house of hope. I'd rather do that than support a dilapidated house of despair."

Community Planning:
A Way out of Addiction

A MAN BURST THROUGH THE DOOR OF THE SAGAMOK Youth Centre, startling the group seated around a flip chart.

"Help me, help me," he cried. "I've been drinking for a month. I haven't eaten. I can't sleep. Help me."

The twenty or so people in the room, including me, didn't stir. It was as if we were watching a play. The elderly man had appeared right on cue—everyone had just been talking about the Anishnawbe reserve's drinking problem. But the man's distress was very real. As he wept he reverted to speaking his native language, though one English word got attention. When he said "detox," some people around me sprang into action.

"I'll call Orion Southwind," a workshop participant said, leaving the room to phone the reserve's addictions worker.

"We'll take a fifteen-minute break," said the workshop leader, Michael Bopp.

The 1,400 people of the Sagamok Anishnawbek First Nation, a reserve 120 kilometres west of Sudbury, are involved in a daring social experiment, one that holds out hope for the future of Aboriginal communities across the country. Sitting around flip charts and talking about the future may not seem revolutionary, but the results have been. Five years into its Community Healing and Development Ten-Year Action Plan, Sagamok can boast that 88 per cent of its employees are now sober, including the forty-three-year-old chief, Paul Eshkakogan.

"At first I was pretty skeptical about community planning," Eshkakogan told me. "I think it was because of the amount of work that was involved. It was like looking at a mountain and saying, how are we ever going to get up there, start climbing that mountain and start to address the work?"

But now he's sold on it.

"Things are improving," Eshkakogan said. "I can see it in the people. There is healing going on, there is growth. Even myself. I've gone on somewhat of a journey. Alcohol and drugs are not a part of my life anymore, nor part of my family's. Our focus is on the children. I think that's where this whole community healing has to start."

Thirty residents of the reserve would soon graduate from the "Moving towards Wellness" course designed by Michael Bopp and his wife Judie. The graduates would, in turn, teach what they've learned to others in the community.

The Bopps have been honing their skills in community development for thirty years, first in Third World countries and now with Aboriginal people across North America. Twenty years ago they teamed up with a dynamic Dakota Sioux named Phil Lane Jr., and since then they have built a reputation in

Canada's Aboriginal communities as compassionate, informed people with practical solutions to help ease suffering. Their non-profit institute, the Four Worlds Centre for Development Learning, is based on four founding principles: development from within; no vision, no development; individual and community development are connected; and learning is required. As their Web site describes, the name Four Worlds was chosen because of the cultural and spiritual significance of the medicine wheel. The four cardinal points of the wheel can be used to explain the complex reality of personal and community development. In the first module of "Moving towards Wellness," people begin with themselves, exploring how they learn best and what kind of personal growth and healing is needed in their own lives. In the second module they learn about conflict resolution and human relations. The third module teaches what's needed for community development and nation building. The fourth covers program development.

Sagamok entrepreneur Levi Southwind brought the Bopps to his community after reading their book, *Recreating the World: A Practical Guide to Building Sustainable Communities,* and attending a summer course at their Cochrane, Alberta, institute.

Southwind grew up in Sagamok at the worst of times. When he reached adulthood in the 1960s, almost everyone his age was an alcoholic. He was one, too. Given his difficult childhood, he found it hard to believe in himself. "In residential school it was always a shameful thing to be an Indian person," he told me. "I went to school, I did all the things that I was told to do, and yet when I graduated out of high school, which was very uncommon for our community, with honours no less, I could not get employment. Why was that? I was too naive in terms of the Indian world and the non-Indian world. I just figured maybe there was no work."

Southwind migrated south to Toronto. During the course of a career in construction and band council administration, he picked up many skills that have proven valuable to his community over the years. Sobriety was one of them. "I remember coming for a visit in the community. I went home and people were trying to pass me the bottle and said, here, come drink with us. I said, no, I quit drinking. They said, oh, what's the matter, you too good for us now? That kind of thing. So there's a lot of pressure. If you can't work your way through that, then you don't beat them, you join them."

Southwind did join them for a while, but he was urged back into sobriety by a local NNADAP worker, a woman who'd known him all his life and wanted to put his talents to work. After receiving addiction treatment at Elliot Lake, Southwind began to do whatever he could to move his people towards a better life. He started up a number of enterprises, believing employment would encourage more community members to become sober. He grew discouraged, however, when the businesses failed, largely because sobriety wasn't widely embraced.

"Well, you certainly have to have a lot of patience," he says about that time in his life. "I kept saying, I've had enough of this. I'm going, I don't need any more of this. I can get along well by myself. I'd go and rest for a little while and I'd come back saying, okay, where did we leave off here? Let's keep going. That's having, I guess, compassion and love for your people."

Comprehensive community development—the strategy promoted by the Four Worlds Centre—harnesses that love and turns the commitment of sober Aboriginals to the benefit of everyone else. Levi Southwind applied to the Aboriginal

Healing Foundation for funding to bring the Bopps to Sag-amok. By 2001 the funding was in place, and the healing program took off.

"I know in my own heart and mind Michael and Judie are the best in the business," he says. "They go all over the world helping communities. When they come here, they're not doing everything themselves and creating dependency. They're help-ing transfer knowledge and skills to the community so we can become more self-reliant. There was an attitude certainly, in this community, that things had been going on for so long there was no use trying to do anything about it. Community development is development of people. It opens up their minds to realize that change is possible and puts them on a learning curve to see how that could be done."

The first part of the Bopps' strategy is to get a community to reflect upon its past, in order to determine what's needed to succeed. According to Michael Bopp, this is crucial. "The com-munity story is done by gathering people up in a large meeting and sitting them in small circles and asking them to talk about what life is like for them. What's going on for children? For youth, women, elders? What's going on in politics? Econom-ics? What's happening in all different aspects of life—spiritual, cultural? What's it like to live in Sagamok? What was it like in the past? What can we learn from that past, about how things have unfolded? What would it be like in the future if it was really good? So you have a past, present and future perspec-tive on the situation, a kind of description through story, of what life would be like in a healthier place. What you're doing is exposing the community's thinking about itself. All of that is self-reflective for the community. From there, we sit with community people and make kind of a general framework of priorities, things that need to be done in order to bring the community forward."

The Sagamok community story revealed that half the reserve's population was under the age of twenty-five, and that 80 to 90 per cent of the youth were drinking, using drugs and getting into trouble through attempted suicides, accidents and failure in school.

"The people told us their young people were not becoming the kind of whole, happy, healthy adults they want them to be," Bopp said. "There was no economy. All the money was transfer money. The government's economic development program was training people for jobs where there weren't any jobs. The community had no resources to create jobs. The governance system is structured after municipal governments in Britain and North America. It's not their traditional way of governing. They had a clan system. So they discussed what life might be like if they governed themselves that way again. The primary priorities were addressing community wellness—alcohol and sexual abuse, family violence, a mistrust, undermining one another, all the things that were hurting individuals, but also preventing the community from moving forward and generating enough unity to begin to address key social and economic issues. A framework for action was then drawn up, and we began to work systematically over the next number of years to try to implement some of that stuff. Our job at Four Worlds was to figure out what they have to learn here and how we can help them to learn it."

In the first phase of the program, people in Sagamok participated in 300 door-to-door surveys and in focus groups and training sessions. Fifty youth were taken on a retreat to collect their ideas and thoughts. A community newspaper was created, and high school students took a cultural awareness course aimed at boosting their self-esteem.

Best of all, a blueprint for the community's future was drawn up. Sagamok's ten-year community healing and development plan reads like a constitution. An excerpt from the plan reveals what lies at its heart: "Unity in the Community, peace of mind and personal well-being will be distinguishing features of life in Sagamok. These will be rooted in the spiritual practices, cultural traditions and a deeply felt relationship with each person and with God the Creator. Those who follow the Anishnawbe way will not be ashamed of their beliefs, medicines, ceremonies and customs."

Trained people will be needed to carry out the plan, and that's where the Bopps' workshop the afternoon I attended came in. Most of the participants provided social services to the community, and they were discussing the "determinants of health" and ways to make children on the reserve safer.

"When are the children least safe?" Michael Bopp asked the dozen people seated with him around the flip chart.

"On cheque days," said Albert Eshkakogan without hesitation. "Whenever money comes into the community, children are less safe because their parents may go drinking."

"The band council sponsors events that sell alcohol to raise money," added Violet Boissoneau, who was seated across from Eshkakogan. "We make children less safe then."

Bopp wrote what was said on the flip chart. After more discussion, the group drew up a recommendation that alcohol no longer be sold at community events. They knew their recommendation would become band council policy, because the local government is obliged to follow the plan's "pathways to the future."

"Children will grow up in families which are free of addictions, violence and abuse," the plan states. "The community will make healthy children and families a priority."

Levi Southwind moved around the makeshift classroom at the Sagamok Youth Centre like a proud new father.

"Brainstorming like this forces us to rethink what we take for granted," he said during a break. "We get locked into unhealthy ways of thinking and behaving. Training helps us to learn new ways and gets us excited about making change."

Other participants confirmed his observations. "It's certainly not what I expected," said Marilyn Southwind (a relative by marriage to Levi). "I thought it was about the community, but I'm learning a lot about myself. I thought I was a good parent, but I can see things I'm doing that are not so good, ways I can improve. I realize there are issues in my life I need to work on."

The effects of community development are already being felt, Levi Southwind told me. In 2003, those who helped to draw up the community plan estimated that 70 per cent of males in Sagamok, 60 per cent of the females and 80 to 90 per cent of the youth abused alcohol or drugs. Southwind believed a new survey would find that number revised downwards, and that alcohol abuse had become less socially acceptable than it was before.

"I don't see the people coming home drunk, falling down anymore," he said. "Very seldom do I see signs of physical abuse, which used to be commonplace years ago. I grew up with that violence. It's seldom seen nowadays."

The Bopps, Phil Lane Jr. and Julian Norris conducted a study for Corrections Canada in 2001 looking at what six Aboriginal communities in Canada with lower rates of addiction had in common. The report they produced, "Mapping the Healing Journey" is written with compassion and a deep understanding of the tremendous challenges Aboriginal people face. The report does not downplay the difficulties of instituting change: "Aboriginal communities that have been traumatized display a fairly predictable pattern of collective dysfunction in the form of rampant backbiting and gossip, perpetual social and political conflict and in-fighting, a tendency to pull down the good work of anyone who arises to serve the community, political corruption, lack of accountability and transparency in governance, widespread suspicion and mistrust between people, chronic inability to unite and work together to solve critical human problems, competition and turf wars between programs, a general sense of alienation and disengagement from community affairs by most people (what's the use?), a climate of fear and intimidation surrounding those who hold power and a general lack of progress and success in community initiatives and enterprises (which often seem to self-destruct)."

However, the report continues, "We now know that those patterns too, like their counterparts at the individual and family levels, can be transformed through persistent and effective processes of community healing and development. It is abundantly clear that Aboriginal nations cannot progress as long as this pattern of recycling trauma and dysfunction, generation after generation, is allowed to continue. Something is needed to interrupt the cycle and to introduce new patterns of living that lead to sustainable human wellbeing and prosperity."

During a workshop break, Michael Bopp sat down with me to explain how the Four Worlds training program works. "The whole community must get involved in creating a common vision, with hope for the future. This can't be imposed from the outside. We've learned that it is essential for a core group of people within the community to develop both the knowledge and skill to help lead the process. When there's strong leadership supporting that process, and when personal, cultural, economic, political and social development are worked on at the same time, communities have the best chance to heal. Professionals can come in to train community members, but then they have to go away and leave the community to do the work."

The Sagamok reserve is a beautiful place. The road into the reserve leads past a natural rock formation that looks like an "Indian" head in profile, with a mouth opened as if shouting. According to Levi Southwind, some people believe that a Windigo, or trickster, is locked up inside the rock. The road follows the curve of the Spanish River most of the way. Sagamok's natural beauty shows what this part of Ontario must have looked like before the establishment of the Elliot Lake uranium mine, Sudbury's huge nickel mine, and all the forest cutting that keeps the Spanish River Pulp and Paper company going in nearby Espanola. Many of the houses on the reserve are set in among a forest of elegant maple trees, and maple syrup is produced in season.

On a driving tour of the reserve, Levi Southwind and I passed some failed economic development projects. There was an abandoned log house, built as part of a training course; no one has built another log house since. Work was started on a marina and a summer cottage development, but they didn't take off, either. Southwind told me a connection was missing between the projects and the people.

"Alcohol and drugs are not the only addictions that we have in our communities, or dysfunctions or things that need to be worked on," he said. "We have a whole series of things. When we put the cap on the bottle and sober up, we begin to realize there's a whole slew of other things that need to be addressed. You can say that the use of alcohol or drugs is a symptom of something deeper."

Brenda Rivers, Sagamok's band manager, believes the malaise that has kept her community down is something deeply internal, having to do with feelings of inferiority and what psychologists call "anomie," societal alienation that leads to the erosion and abandonment of moral and social codes. A course that Rivers took in 1998 changed her life. Called "What Was Never Told," it was devised by Bob Antone, executive director of the KiiKeeWaNiiKaan Southwest Regional Healing Lodge near Muncey, Ontario, and Jim Dumont of Laurentian University.

"I didn't know my people's history," Rivers told me when we met. "I only knew of our failures, not our successes. I didn't know about the events that led up to our problems today. We blamed ourselves."

Armed with more self-confidence, Rivers began studying at Ryerson University for a degree in public administration and governance. She told me she once would have been too intimidated even to do a media interview, but she'd recently briefed Ontario's attorney general on what's happening in Sagamok.

Rivers sits most days in front of two computers that contain the spreadsheets she has created to standardize the band's financial reporting systems. She is confident the reserve's high management standards will soon qualify it for recognition from the International Organization for Standardization (ISO), she hopes this will attract outside investors.

"If people are going to come off welfare, we need outside investment," Rivers said. "There's none at all here now."

The large boreal forest Sagamok is set in looks like a national park. Some people feel isolated, but Chief Paul Eshka-kogan told me that has more to do with poor self-esteem and poverty than with geographic location.

"We want to have manufacturing here in the community," he said. "I think if industry were to come knocking on our door today and say to me, Chief, we have 200 jobs for you, I'd have to say, sure, we'll take them, but you've got to give us time to heal our labour force. The jobs are out there, they're out there in forestry and mining, fisheries and the service sector, but our people need the motivation to go back out there and compete for those jobs. Part of that motivation is healing. They're just carrying around so much right now, and I think this process will help them to deal with the problems they have, to get back on the right path."

About 100 families on the Sagamok reserve receive social assistance. When the community plan is fully implemented, people will be encouraged to come off that assistance and receive money for training and higher education instead.

"This is not something that will be forced on people," Brenda Rivers assured me. "But we think people will want to do this. We will offer career counselling to help people realize their dreams."

According to a teenager I met hitchhiking one day, young people on the reserve are learning a work ethic along with community pride. "I had a summer job in community plan-ning. We went to school to learn our history," she told me. "If we were late or didn't show up, we didn't get paid."

The goal of the Sagamok's ambitious ten-year plan is to cre-ate a vibrant citizenry ready to take advantage of economic and educational opportunities that exist near the reserve. Training courses like the one that Michael Bopp is facilitating will earn some of the participants credits from Algoma College. There's a lot to do in the next five years and a lot at stake.

There's been one significant triumph already. In the fall of 2007, the reserve was successful in getting ISO certification from the Quality Management Institute (QMI). This means that all of the finances they administer, from health care to education and planning, meet the most stringent guidelines set internationally for a financial organization. Wendy Titford, the president of QMI, told a local newspaper that only 4,000 companies worldwide have achieved this certification, and Sagamok is the second Aboriginal community in Canada to do so. (The first was the Membertou First Nation in Nova Scotia in 2002.) Brenda Rivers was asked to speak to more than 600 financial officers from First Nations communities across Canada at the 2007 meeting of the National Aboriginal Financial Officers Association, who wanted to know how this could be done. ISO certification is the best quality assurance any business could ask for if it wants to partner with Sagamok, and the community is looking to the future.

Implementing a National Strategy

THE VIEW WAS BREATHTAKING FROM PATRICK KELLY'S high-rise corner office at Indian and Northern Affairs Canada in downtown Vancouver. When I met with him in 2006, Kelly was INAC's Director of Planning and Communication for the B.C. region; today he's a private consultant. At the time, Kelly told me that he and his counterpart in Atlantic Canada, Dan Yarymowich, were the first federal employees ever to hold positions that promoted community planning as a priority in Aboriginal communities. He called that a "tremendous oversight."

Kelly is from a B.C. First Nations community called Leq'á:mel, part of the Sto:lo nation. In 1970, he became the community's first high school graduate. His mother was once a band councillor, and he remembered watching her at home, with files spread out on the kitchen table, filling out report after report to Indian and Northern Affairs Canada.

"The reports she wrote were serving administrative purposes that were often disconnected from the real needs of our people," he told me. "She spent so much time and energy satisfying these administrative needs, she didn't have the energy and time to do what she really wanted to do, create new business and employment opportunities. This was very frustrating for my mother."

Much the same system is in place today, Kelly said, and he felt requiring Aboriginal communities to complete between 100 and 160 reports for his department annually was counterproductive. "In this process, communities don't have a way to express what they really need and want. There's nothing there that people can translate into action. That's where I think the whole process of community planning becomes a critical tool, to translate the strong desire that communities and people have to get things done."

At an Ottawa public policy conference sponsored by the University of Western Ontario in March 2006, Kelly announced an initiative he hoped would make a fundamental change in the way his department did business. Presenting a paper entitled "Investing in Change: First Nations Comprehensive Community Planning," he told delegates that Indian and Northern Affairs Canada was working on a major new strategy for funding Aboriginal communities.

According to the 2006 report of Canada's Auditor General, thirty-four federal organizations fund 360 programs and services for First Nations, Inuit and Métis communities. A staggering 60,000 reports are filed annually to apply and account for that funding.

"In the past, planning has been largely driven by those external to the First Nations community," Kelly told delegates to the conference. "This often resulted in a plan that was neither relevant nor sustainable. In some cases, it is a process that has hindered community planning and priority setting, and it has not necessarily produced sustainable results for either the First Nations community or for the department."

Kelly wanted to see many made-in-Ottawa programs eliminated, he told me in Vancouver, with funding channelled through a single department dedicated to community planning. "By involving and engaging [band] membership directly, a vision for the future and a plan to guide development are created that truly reflect the community's values, needs and goals, which ultimately leads to a more relevant and more sustainable community plan," he said.

Kelly liked what he'd seen in the B.C. communities where community planning had already gotten started, he told me. "It is such a huge boost to the emotions, to the spirit of the people when they see that someone has actually acted on one of their suggestions. They become much more enthused, more trusting of their leadership and the other people working for the community. It really has a very profound and positive effect."

Community consultations in Lytton, B.C., in 2003 united three First Nations reserves that were geographically divided and got them working together for the first time in a combined firefighting strategy and in economic development. According to Kelly, it didn't cost his department much to get the process rolling. "We provided food for the elders, and there were snacks and healthy food provided at meetings. Small things like this unleash a huge amount of goodwill and help ensure that people show up, share their ideas, say what they've been holding in for some time."

Following such meetings, Kelly said, a government

department can help by providing technical assistance and training in the community to allow residents to put their ideas into action.

Atlantic Canada has the highest percentage of First Nations communities involved in community planning, according to Dan Yarymowich. "In the three years that federal government departments and communities in the region have been working to implement these plans, we have changed our organizations, our ways of doing business and our relationships," he told delegates to the Ottawa conference. Yarymowich reported that half the Aboriginal communities in his region had drawn up community plans already, and they were slowly starting to implement them. He encouraged researchers attending the conference to study the process, expressing the hope that positive reports could speed things up.

A National Comprehensive Community Planning Strategy has been prepared by INAC, Patrick Kelly told me, but it will take years to change old habits. It's as difficult to adjust the way federal government departments do things as it is to change destructive habits in Aboriginal communities. "The federal government is a large and complex organization, so it's probably not realistic for us to think that we can do this as quickly as I'd like," Kelly admitted. The provinces have responsibility for some aspects of First Nations governance and will need to get involved as well. What's needed most, Kelly said, is the political will.

"There's certainly a willingness on the part of the B.C. government to join Canada and the First Nations leadership in examining these kinds of creative solutions," he told me. "It's now a matter of finding practical methods by which that can actually be realized."

One very practical proposed solution is to have one government department, preferably the Treasury Board, fund First Nations, Metis and Inuit communities, rather than channelling money through the thirty different departments that do it now. The funding should be for a five-year period as well, rather than going year by year as is done currently. "Aboriginal communities need to be able to define the future for their communities for the next twenty to thirty years," Patrick Kelly said. "This is not possible with short-term program funds. A comprehensive community planning approach, however, provides a community with a long-term plan that can act as the bridge or the delivery mechanism that connects the sustainability principles, the community's fundamental values, with the quality of life objectives: what the community and its members need for daily living."

Community planning enthusiasts such as Kelly and Yarymowich don't think this way of doing things will be more expensive. There's a good chance, in fact, that this will be a cheaper alternative to the inefficient way billions of dollars are now spent annually to fund the status quo.

Michael Bopp of the Four Worlds Centre supports the INAC initiatives, but he doesn't believe civil servants should be the ones to deliver comprehensive community planning in Aboriginal communities, at least not until they receive the right kind of training. Bureaucracies such as the one set up to deliver the Labrador Innu Comprehensive Healing Strategy usually make more work for themselves than for the people they are supposedly serving, he told me, and this trend could just lead to the "same old same old."

"Community planning in Aboriginal communities will mean a shift towards building the capacity of community people to lead and sustain the healing work," Bopp stated emphatically. "This requires a shift in focus, from professionals as the sole providers of healing services to professionals training key community volunteers and providing backup support, especially as related to difficult or advanced healing problems."

Patrick Kelly now works from his home, advising First Nations communities in British Columbia how to take part in comprehensive community planning. He believes his time is better spent this way, and there's little time to waste.

"We're still quite a ways from a system-wide approach, certainly," he says today. "I think the urgency is that we can't lose any more generations of people. It's a benefit for all Canadians when Aboriginal people start taking care of themselves and contribute to the betterment of society. I think Aboriginal people have a huge amount to offer Canadian society. We are an untapped wealth of human resources."

The Aboriginal Healing Foundation

IT WAS A SHORT BUT BUMPY ATV RIDE TO THE FOREST clearing on the Wanipigow (Hollow Water) reserve where Gabriel Hall keeps forty dogs, a mix of breeds. The animals started barking before our vehicle came into view, the noise ricocheting off the tall spindly trees that provide shade for this unruly settlement of dog houses. Hall, a thirty-two-year-old Manitoba Cree, is the wilderness coordinator for Wanipigow's Community Holistic Circle Healing (CHCH) process. His work is paid for by a unique Canadian foundation that was created to heal the damage done to Aboriginal society by residential schools.

The policy of assimilating Canada's diverse Aboriginal population was first articulated in 1857 by legislation called *An Act of Gradual Civilization*. As the years passed, the federal government's assimilation policy became more and more heavy-handed. A law passed in 1920 required Aboriginal parents to send children between the ages of seven and fifteen to residential schools. These schools were intentionally constructed far from the children's home reserves, so that enforcement of the law would be less of a problem. There were eighty residential schools, most of them located in western Canada. Several hundred thousand Aboriginal children are believed to have attended the schools; during the peak years of their operation, the 1930s and '40s, 10,000 children a year were sent away to residential school. The last school closed in 1996, and there are an estimated 86,000 former residential school students alive today.

Mary Sillett, now mayor of Hopedale, Nunatsiavut, was a member of the Royal Commission on Aboriginal Peoples. Sillett was born in Labrador, and she'd had a positive educational experience herself at a small Inuit boarding school. She knew little about residential schools in the rest of the country until she heard testimony from former students during the hearings the commission held across the country in the early 1990s. What she learned shocked her. "We thought we'd hear complaints about the loss of land and about political problems," she told me, "but the testimony that overwhelmed us came from people who'd gone to residential school. It was very emotional."

Many former students told the commission that they had been physically and sexually abused at the school. Residential schools also robbed them of normal family life and of their native languages and cultural traditions. The result, for many, has been a lifetime of addiction and mental health problems.

The Aboriginal Healing Foundation was created in 1998, on the Royal commission's recommendation, to deal with this painful legacy. The foundation was given a ten-year mandate and $350 million to help heal communities and individuals negatively impacted by the schools. The healing fund awarded 1,345 grants for projects in remote First Nations and Inuit communities, providing employment for thousands of people in places where jobs are scarce. More importantly, it has kick-started healing in troubled Aboriginal communities. In Wanipigow, the money received from the foundation for the CHCH process has been used creatively, to help not only people directly affected by sexual abuse but those impacted by the intergenerational effects of residential school.

The morning I arrived, Gabriel Hall was expecting a visitor, an eight-year-old boy who had to atone for attacking his school principal in an outburst of anger. Hall knew what lay behind the boy's troubles.

"He's been taken away from his parents due to neglect," Hall told me. "I believe I can help him."

Wanipigow's CHCH employees had recommended some serious face time between the boy and Hall's dogs, and Hall was going to assign him to paint a name on each doghouse.

"He's going to paint signs with the dogs' names so he knows each dog is an individual. That will help him understand he's a valued individual, too," Hall told me. The boy would do the work after school with Hall, who is a strong role model; he's the father of several boys himself. Discipline would be required to complete the task, and Hall believed important emotional connections would be made. "All these dogs have different traits and qualities. I'm hoping he'll bond with one or two of them. I got some from kennels where they'd been abused."

Hall trains other youth to care for the dogs and also prepares them for sled excursions. In the winter of 2005, 600 people were taken by dogsled to a wilderness camp, 200 of them students from the local school. In January 2007, the community became part of the North American sled dog circuit and hosted its first race, inviting teams from across Canada and the United States to participate. Hall keeps his focus, however, on the children.

"I teach them how to cook bannock on an open fire, set snares, run the dog team," Hall said. "I learned all this from my grandpa. He used dogs for trapping and he raced them. That kind of stuck around with me."

This is a dream job for him, Hall told me. People on the reserve feel lucky to have him, too. He and the dogs have already made a difference.

"I've seen some pretty good changes," Hall said. "I keep in contact with the principal and teachers to see what kind of effect it's had on the youth, and they say it's really helped raise their spirits. It's given them something else to talk about in school."

Something other than suicide: almost everyone on this side of Lake Winnipeg, and farther north, has lost a relative or friend in that way. There's also extreme poverty in Wanipigow, and Hall's dog project enriches the social environment. When we spoke, Hall was concerned about how he'd keep the project going once the healing foundation funds run out in March 2010.

There's nothing quite like the Aboriginal Healing Foundation anywhere in the world. A directory in the lobby of a nondescript office building in downtown Ottawa lists the names of dozens of organizations, only one of which has the ambitious mandate of rebuilding Aboriginal societies. The foundation's eighth-floor offices would be a sterile set of rooms were it not for the warmth provided by soft lighting and Aboriginal artwork.

At its inception, the AHF appointed Dr. Gail Valaskakis, a former dean of arts at Montreal's Concordia University and founder of that city's Native Friendship Centre, as director of research. The publications produced during her time in the position are kept in a large room where books are stacked floor to ceiling, all of them related to the impact residential schools have had on generations of people. The output has been prodigious, and when I met her Valaskakis expressed pride that so much of it had been done by Aboriginals. She dropped the names of dozens of Aboriginal scholars and their research specialties into our conversation, offering their contact information from a well-worn address book that she kept close at hand. "We've witnessed the birth of an Aboriginal intellectual movement in Canada," she told me with satisfaction.

Non-Aboriginal researchers and consultants have made countless millions over the years writing about social problems in Aboriginal communities, but their research rarely benefits the people affected. The Aboriginal writers the foundation has published are deeply committed to their communities, and they want to apply their research on the ground. Bill Mussell, for example, is a Sto:lo man who chairs the Native Mental Health Association of Canada. He has written a resource guide for Aboriginal men. Meant to be used at workshops, it offers practical guidance to communities and groups that want to make change. Mussell believes cultural insecurity, particularly among males, causes alcohol abuse as well as depression and destructive behaviour. "Creating conditions and situations to promote the development of a positive personal and cultural identity is the core challenge," he writes in *Warrior-Caregivers: Understanding the Challenges and Healing of First Nations Men*. "From 1950 to the present, I witnessed the following changes: from relative self-sufficiency and team-work to relative dependency and absence of teamwork; from mutual support in most families to reliance upon government service systems." His work is aimed at reversing the process.

There has been a lot of excitement too about the foundation's work in Aboriginal communities. A click of the mouse on the AHF's Web site brings up a map of Canada for each year of funding, with red dots indicating communities where a project has received support. Jake Gearheard manages the project under way in Clyde River, Nunavut. He explained from his small office at the Ilisaqsivik Society in 2006 that the group had received $724,000 from the foundation over the past four years. With that money, Gearheard was able to hire seven people, one of whom was a trained psychological counsellor, the community's first.

"We do land-based healing projects," he explained. "We travel great distances to places that have significance to our clients. We take their families and spend as long as a week hearing stories, many of them about loss since so much change has happened in peoples' lives. They talk about things they never talk about back in the community. The land brings back memories they've buried. The children and grandchildren learn what life was like before people were uprooted, either to be hospitalized in the South or resettled somewhere else."

The Ilisaqsivik Society also sponsors women's gatherings, Gearheard told me. "When the women are sitting together, say sewing, they open up more. It's been an important part of their healing."

The foundation's support has provided an important impetus for healing in Clyde River. Rapid change, residential school and disease outbreaks have created a lot of grief. There were eleven suicides between 1999 and 2003, a lot for a community of just 800. Releasing that grief is part of the healing process, though sometimes it can be too raw to witness.

"I videotaped a session recently," Gearheard told me, "but I don't think we'll show it to anyone. It's very hard to describe the effect of what's happened to people here to anyone who has not lived it."

Gearheard also praised the Healing Foundation for the way it funds projects. "The funding is multi-year," he explained, "and that gives my staff more job security and allows us to do long-term planning. Grants from other government departments are year by year, so we're never sure they'll be renewed. We lose staff that way."

Michael DeGagné is the AHF's executive director. He is a member of the Couchiching Saltaux Ojibway First Nation and was born in Fort Frances, Ontario. DeGagné cut his teeth in the field of healing as a youth worker, where he learned that keeping children busy was one of the best ways to keep them out of trouble. His education and his ease in the non-Aboriginal world equipped him for a career in Ottawa, and DeGagné worked previously for Health Canada, as director of accounting operations, and as a senior negotiator for Indian and Northern Affairs Canada.

"When I was with government, if I asked people to report a surplus or tell me if things were not going well, they didn't, because they knew the funding would disappear," he told me. "But the foundation has worked hard to gain trust, and we've said, tell us if we're doing it wrong. Tell us if things aren't going well and then we'll make it better. I think that's why we've got a great success rate. People come to us honestly, because they know that we're not going to burn them."

The Friendship Centre in Hinton, Alberta, is another foundation success story. The centre has pioneered a therapeutic program in the community to break the destructive cycle of incest. John Higgerty is Hinton's Crown prosecutor and his wife, Lisa, runs the Mamowichihitowin (All of Us Working Together) program at the friendship centre. John Higgerty is notified whenever disclosure of incest is made, and then he must determine whether the perpetrator is eligible for the Mamowichihitowin process.

"I don't think there's any higher rate of incest offences in Aboriginal communities," he told me after a presentation at the Healing Our Spirit Worldwide conference. "The real point to this entire conference is that Aboriginal people are far more ready, far more prepared, to deal with the problems of their society than mainstream communities are. I am thoroughly convinced of this after twenty-five years as a lawyer, twenty-two of that as a government prosecutor."

Programs such as those at Mamowichihitowin and Wanipigow demonstrate how changing people through therapy and community programs is not only cheaper than jail, but can be much more effective.

The community of Wabaseemoong used the money it received from the Aboriginal Healing Foundation to recover the remains of their dead, whose graves had been destroyed by the flooding created by Ontario Hydro's projects. "The Aboriginal Healing Foundation has really helped us," Charles McDonald told me. As Wabaseemoong's wellness worker, he knew perhaps better than anyone how upset people had been to find human remains along the riverbanks near their former communities.

Those connected to the AHF don't want the important work they've started to stop when the government money runs out.

The initial grant of $350 million was allocated until March 2008, ten years after the foundation's creation. Some additional projects have been funded until 2012, thanks to $125 million provided by the Residential School Settlement Agreement that came into effect in the fall of 2007. The foundation board of directors, led by Georges Erasmus, doesn't think there's been enough time to fulfill the mission the foundation was given: "to encourage and support Aboriginal people in building and reinforcing sustainable healing processes that address the legacy of physical and sexual abuse in the residential school system, including intergenerational impacts."

In 2006, the foundation's board approached the federal government with an idea for sustainable funding. It asked for a one-time endowment of $600 million that would be invested, with the proceeds used to keep the foundation's work going for several more decades. Gail Valaskakis presented details of the plan to the Senate Committee on Mental Health, Mental Illness and Addiction that same year.

"We estimate that it takes a community on average ten years to reach out, dismantle denial, create safety and engage participants in the therapeutic healing process," she told the committee. "The projects funded by the Aboriginal Healing Foundation have played a critical role in this. About one quarter of all Aboriginal people in Canada lost their connection to family because of residential school. They or their parents and grandparents were institutionalized during childhood. Many were sexually abused in school by the authorities who ran them . . . If invested at a 5 per cent rate of return, with a 2.5 per cent inflation rate, the endowment would make $28.7 million available to distribute to Aboriginal communities for the next thirty years."

"A healthy community, a healed community, is the lynch-pin for better use of all kinds of government money," the AHF's Michael DeGagné told me. Because of this, DeGagné is concerned all that has been achieved through the founda-tion's support might be dismantled. "We thought, if we did a good enough job and showed the government that we're not going to give away the store, they'd let us continue. We have an accountability regime that is outstanding, second to none. We cooperate with the Treasury Board, we cooperate with the Auditor General. We follow our negotiated contribution agree-ment to the letter, and we actually think that this is the way to help communities heal. It's faster, cheaper and more responsive than anything a big government department might try to do."

Despite the strong case the foundation made, however, their request for an endowment fell on deaf ears. There was no mention of it in the Senate Committee's final report, nor did it attract a champion in government. Like the Kelowna Accord, the AHF's proposal didn't get past go.

Today, the Aboriginal Healing Foundation is in the pro-cess of winding down its work. There's a stark line across the centre of its Web site home page: "Please note that the AHF is not providing any funding for new projects." Gail Valaskakis didn't get the full decade she believed was needed to create a solid impetus for change in Aboriginal communities; her life was cut short by cancer in the winter of 2007. The room in which we met will be renamed the Gail Guthrie Valaskakis Reading Room at an official ceremony in the spring of 2008. Michael DeGagné, Georges Erasmus and the rest of the AHF team are working hard to make sure the research nurtured by Valaskakis is translated into action. In 2000, they created the Legacy of Hope Foundation, a national charitable organization mandated to educate Canadians about the impact of residential schools on Aboriginal society. The AHF has created an exhibition of photographs, original classroom texts, maps and other information related to residential schools called "Where Are the Children: Healing the Legacy of Residential Schools." The exhibit has travelled extensively in western Canada, and its accompanying Web site, www.wherearethechildren.ca, recreates the experience of attending one of these schools from a child's point of view. The team's energy will also go into making sure the new Truth and Reconciliation Commission has the broadest possible impact.

Marcel Hardisty of Wanipigow thinks the federal government has made a big mistake in closing down the Aboriginal Healing Foundation. He considers its creation one of the best things Canada has ever done for Aboriginal people. "It provided financial support to do meaningful wellness programming in the community," he told me. "In our community we're certainly making good use of that funding, because we are tapping our traditional knowledge, our traditional skills and making that part of our therapy. For example, the wilderness therapy is developing to the point where we can actually create a revenue-generating business through eco tourism and other related ventures with dogs and people."

The foundation's approach was vastly different from that of most government departments, Hardisty said. "Their funding guidelines were less restrictive and more conducive to supporting local initiatives. What we get from government departments is more of 'give them enough money to ensure they don't succeed'; that's what it feels like. Take the CHCH process. That whole approach works. But the federal government and the province provide just enough money to have a bare-bones operation going here. When it comes to incarcerating people, they seem to have all the money in the world. Every year we wonder, who's going to make the decision first, the federal government or the province? Who's going to provide the financial support? That's always been the issue year by year. Will we have money to continue?"

Lessons from Old Crow

THE PRIDE AND JOY OF CANADA'S MOST REMOTE, AND healthiest, Aboriginal community is plain to see on the community's Web site. Each year, at *www.oldcrow.ca,* the community posts photos of its high school graduates. In 2006, the photos showed four young men and two young women leaning against a building. The young men wore their caps and gowns with flair; one had his arms crossed and his head cocked as though challenging the world. One young woman had her arm around an elderly Gwich'in man. Her grandfather, perhaps.

Six high school graduates from a community of 300 may not seem like a big accomplishment. But the Yukon reserve of Old Crow has no roads connecting it to anywhere else. The community is 200 kilometres above the Arctic Circle, close to the Alaskan border. After university many of these graduates may want to return home; despite its remoteness, Old Crow is a good place to live. There hasn't been a suicide in Old Crow since 1996. Even that death may have been accidental.

"We might have prevented it had we been able to act more quickly," Chief Joe Linklater explained.

One academic study is always cited when the subject of Canada's high Aboriginal suicide rate is raised. The study, conducted in British Columbia by professors Chris Lalonde and Michael Chandler in 1998, is entitled "Cultural Continuity as a Hedge against Suicide in Canada's First Nations." The professors looked for what made communities with low suicide rates different from more troubled communities. They learned that the healthiest communities maintain their cultural traditions and have a high proportion of people who speak their traditional languages. These communities have something else in common, too: most are self-governing.

Old Crow has had self-government since 1995. Shortly afterwards, Joe Linklater was elected to lead the community at the age of thirty. He's been the chief ever since.

"We've learned more about governance in the past eleven years than in all our years under the *Indian Act*," he told me in 2006. "We've come a huge distance in a short while, especially when you consider the Territorial government is seventy years old, and the Canadian government is 140 years old. I'm proud of what we've accomplished."

Linklater has had a lot of help. Old Crow's governing system is very inclusive. His small band council, just four elected members, administers the community's services. Policy is set by the Elders Council, a tribal court and the General Assembly. You can get a surprising amount of business done that way.

"We held a general assembly this weekend," Linklater said when we spoke, "and forty to fifty people attended. We passed twenty-four resolutions in three hours. There was no yelling or screaming. We got consensus and compromise."

Old Crow is so comfortable with its social health, in fact, that it is seriously considering dropping a fifteen-year-old ban on the consumption and possession of alcohol. Resolution No. 2005-15, passed in 2005 by the General Assembly, says it will "revisit the prohibition of alcohol in Old Crow" and "set up an independent committee to seek community consultation with regard to how the prohibition of alcohol is working and how we as a community can strengthen, alter or abolish the law."

Why consider abolishing a law that seems to be keeping everyone sober?

"There's more alcohol here now than there was fifteen years ago," explained Chief Joe, as the community's leader is affectionately known. Drinking and drug use are not big problems in the community yet, but Linklater is afraid if the bootleggers are not put out of business, the situation may get worse. "I want to stop this criminal element from growing any stronger," Linklater said. "Who knows what else they'll bring in here if they're not stopped?" He is frustrated the police haven't been able to keep drugs and alcohol out of remote fly-in communities such as Old Crow.

Not everyone in town is comfortable with lifting the alcohol ban. When Linklater tried to strike a committee to make recommendations, he couldn't find anyone who was neutral. There were strong feelings all around, so an independent facilitator was hired to chair community meetings until a consensus is reached.

Linklater likes a beer from time to time, he told me, but he won't drink in the community as long as it's illegal. There are others like him who feel Old Crow has enough going for it to make moderate drinking possible. They might be right. Old Crow hasn't suffered the same losses most other Canadian Aboriginal communities have. The habitat of the Porcupine

River caribou herd, the community's main food source, has not been destroyed by a hydroelectric project or a logging operation. Old Crow's isolation has been its saving grace: the people still have their land. The history recorded on the community's Web site is one of continuity: "The name Vuntut Gwitchin derives from our annual muskrat trapping season, where we move approximately 27 miles north from Old Crow, for the months of April to June. The whole area of Crow Flats is covered by small and large lakes...Each family group in Old Crow has their own trapping area, referred to by each family as their or my country. This is an area that has been passed down from generation to generation."

The radiant pictures of the 2006 graduating ceremony also reflect the community's good health and provide insight into the source of the chief's confidence about its future. Elders in floor-length black and red Gwich'in gowns, embroidered with traditional emblems, dance and clap as they lead the students into the community hall for the graduation ceremony. The students are shown with their caps and gowns set aside, relaxing in soft caribou-skin dresses and vests, embroidered in the Gwich'in tradition.

Most Aboriginal communities in Canada celebrate their high school graduates in a big way. These young people are an important measure of a community's success. Saskatchewan sociologist Richard Thatcher believes Aboriginal students who are grounded in their culture yet raised to be comfortable outside of it have the best chance of avoiding addiction and other social problems. Children in Old Crow receive this kind of bicultural education. They follow the same curriculum as children in British Columbia, but there are lots of additions, like the Gwich'in language and traditions.

"The school is an integral part of the community life and

many of the local people work with the students. This is especially true of the elders who spend a lot of time teaching the pupils [their] legends, how to trap, fish and hunt," the Web site explains. Chief Linklater wants to strengthen the students' grasp of math and the sciences with more instruction on the land.

"We'll study biology while out trapping the animals," he told me, "and physics by looking at the property of snow. Our environment is a living laboratory."

The challenges Old Crow's students face have been turned into opportunities. The 2006 graduates, Wade Kaye, Amanda and Travis Frost, Malinda Bruce, Robert Linklater and Floyd McGinnis, had to leave home after grade 9 to attend high school, flying 600 kilometres south to Whitehorse. For three years they lived away from their families, returning only in the summer. But their families never left them. Old Crow is one big extended family, and each fall Gwich'in families living in Whitehorse host a feast to welcome the new batch of high school students. They also provide support throughout the school year to help students cope with life in a larger centre, far from home.

"Strength of culture would be one reason we're a healthy community," Chief Linklater said. "The strength of the Gwich'in language is another. Third, our strong sense of community; everybody looks out for one another. And finally, we all feel ownership of what's going on because we have self-government." Linklater believes his community is on a straight course; alcoholism and other addictions will not be an issue in another generation, he said.

There are some possible threats to the community's stability on the horizon. Global warming is already having an effect, drying up important waterbeds. As well, the United States has been talking about developing oil and gas projects in the sensitive calving and wintering grounds of the Porcupine caribou herd. If these projects go ahead and the herd is affected, the Gwich'in of Old Crow will have to find a way to respond. For now, they're doing everything under their control to prepare their children, in the best possible way, for whatever the future holds.

Conclusion

MARCEL HARDISTY, WANIPIGOW'S ADMINISTRATOR OF social development programs, and Stephen O'Neill, an Ontario Superior court judge, have each worked for years to bring the racism and injustice Aboriginal people face to an end. Although they come from very different backgrounds, the two men are equally passionate in their belief that Canada must honour the promises made when Europeans first came into contact with this country's original inhabitants.

"The public attitude is that the Aboriginal people are a burden to society," Hardisty told me during a conversation at his home on the edge of Lake Winnipeg. "What governments fail to do is educate the public about the real nature of or the real spirit of intent in treaty making. The intent as far as our people understood it, is that we would share the real resources of the land, and that means the raw resources: the royalties from the use of water, minerals, the land and the air. That hasn't been properly recognized within governments and Canadian society. We have a situation where victims are blamed by offenders because, for the most part, the practice of oppression is not just by government, but also by Canadian society."

Hardisty paused. "Young people don't see that it's going to get any better," he said of the epidemic of suicide that surrounds him on reserves in northeastern Manitoba. "We can't afford to allow children and people to die in this way, and it's happening because governments—local, provincial and federal—don't want to look at the real issues."

I met Judge Stephen O'Neill at a Kenora restaurant that overlooks the magnificent scenery of what's known as Lake of the Woods. From the bench, O'Neill is a daily witness to the suffering caused by extreme social problems in Parry Sound and the rest of northern Ontario.

"I think there's a sense that all of these issues are in the past, that they were resolved and that the Aboriginal people have to pick themselves up and move forward," he told me. "But we need to understand history. We need to understand the Crown–First Nation alliances that were made, that first formed this country. We have to have an appreciation of the treaty-making process that allowed for an orderly settlement of the lands of this country."

"What's needed to make Aboriginal lives happier?" I asked the judge.

"The report of the Royal Commission on Aboriginal Peoples said we need to have a reconciliation process. Some people view this as a political problem in Canada, and so they say, let the politicians solve it. Some people will say, let the judges solve this problem. I think it's a mixture of law, politics and history. These issues have been before Canadian people not for five years, not for ten years, not for twenty-five years, but for generations. Justice Dickson said in the 1990 Sparrow decision [which affirmed Aboriginal ancestral and treaty hunting and fishing rights] that for the past century most of the legal rights of Aboriginal people to their land have been virtually ignored. That was a stunning statement for Canada's highest judge to make."

He paused before continuing, glancing out at the waterway below us that once served as a highway for the thousands of Anishnawbe people on reserves that surround Kenora.

"I think we have to spend the next twenty-five or fifty years in this country reconciling ourselves with the Aboriginal people, and they reconciling with us. Most Aboriginal people will tell you, 'We're a sharing people. We're prepared to share.' But unfortunately the history of this country, as noted by judges and politicians, is that it hasn't been a sharing. It's been a top-down relationship, a forced relationship. We've stood on Aboriginal people. We've pushed them down, and they keep coming back up and they say, 'We will move forward with you on a sharing basis, on some sort of a partnership basis.'"

O'Neill does not mince words in talking about what needs to be done.

"I can't understand why some Canadian people don't seem to be getting that message. When we walk into Aboriginal villages and homes and recognize them as good human beings, people to be respected, we have wonderful joint venture projects. Great partnerships. That's what Aboriginal people said should have happened in this country three or four hundred years ago. We have to move forward with them in sharing arrangements and in partnership arrangements. That will take people out of their economic stagnation. That will flow money and work into those communities. That will give people a sense of goodwill and self-esteem. Some say that Aboriginal people should come to the cities, but there are still some minerals to be found in this country. There are still other resources and opportunities to be developed. Those who wish to come will come to the cities. Those who wish to remain on their traditional lands will remain. I think it's time to look at Aboriginal treaty rights, to really respect them as a people and as the original settlers and owners of this great country."

The Assembly of First Nations estimates that there are currently 800 to 1,000 unresolved land claims to be settled with the provinces and the federal government. First Nations communities remain in a state of suspended animation until these agreements are completed. By continuing to disregard Aboriginal rights and treaties, Canadian policies perpetuate the social problems that are tearing Aboriginal families and communities apart.

Canada's Truth and Reconciliation Commission began its five-year mandate in 2008. Commissioners will travel across the country to hear personal testimony about the impact of residential schools on Aboriginal children and adults, and those affected will be honoured at national and community events. Through education and outreach, the commission will work to engage non-Aboriginal Canadians in the reconciliation process. Bob Watts, the commission's executive director, also sees an opportunity for Canada to take leadership internationally through the Truth and Reconciliation process, setting an example for countries that have yet to formally acknowledge the historical oppression of their Aboriginal citizens.

As Canadians—Aboriginal and non-Aboriginal alike—we now have a moment to seize. There have been a lot of losses in Aboriginal society and the depth of grieving is quite intense. Ultimately, healing will come when there is a renewal of hope. What better way to give hope than to let people know that their priorities are national priorities, too.

Recommendations
and Action Plan

1. Create a national agency dedicated to comprehensive Aboriginal community economic development.

In October 2007, Canada's Auditor General, Sheila Fraser, wrote a stinging indictment of how Indian and Northern Affairs Canada has failed to uphold the land claims agreement Canada signed with the Inuvialuit (Inuit) in the western Arctic in 1984.

According to Fraser, in the twenty-three years since the agreement was signed, "The economy of the region has not improved . . . the economic measures have not been met, and the Inuvialuit are falling behind their Northern neighbours . . . The principles expressed by the Inuvialuit, and recognized by Canada in concluding the Agreement, include enabling Inuvialuit to participate equally and meaningfully in the economy and society of Canada's North and of the nation."

Assuring that Aboriginal people are able to participate equally and meaningfully in all aspects of Canadian life is the most important way to prevent, and to promote recovery from, crippling addiction epidemics. Fraser tells us that this hasn't happened for the Inuvialuit because no one at INAC was assigned to implement all the provisions of the land claims agreement. Nor was there a mechanism put in place for doing so. This latest failure by the federal department that manages 65 per cent of Canada's $8-billion budget for Aboriginal programs reinforces what I heard time after time in Aboriginal communities: the weight of this enormous bureaucracy is crushing the aspirations of the people it is meant to serve. INAC is the wrong agency to help Aboriginal communities reach economic and social parity with the rest of Canada, yet it is the only agency set up to do so until self-government is achieved for every Aboriginal community.

What is proposed in this book by people like Patrick Kelly, Levi Southwind, Marcel Hardisty and Michael and Judie Bopp must be given a chance to work. Their vision of grassroots community development, which encompasses social healing, should be put in place as quickly as possible to kick-start Aboriginal independence and self-sufficiency. Community development, if done correctly, will create the conditions necessary for change: hope, jobs, higher educational achievement, greater self-esteem and a reduction in addictive behaviour—partly by dismantling denial, since addressing addiction will be a key part of the process. Comprehensive community development doesn't have to cost taxpayers more, because money can be saved elsewhere—for example, by eliminating the ineffective programs that exist now within INAC and Health Canada, and the high-salaried positions that go with them.

"We recommend a structure a little like that of the Aboriginal Healing Foundation," explains Michael Bopp of the Four Worlds Centre for Development and Learning. "It should be at arm's length from government but initially funded by them. It should consist of a network of small, mobile, regional technical assistance and training centres, supported by a small national team."

Aboriginal employees could initially be mentored by trusted organizations such as Four Worlds, which has substantial experience in community development around the world and an excellent track record in Canada's Aboriginal communities. This is Michael Bopp's vision: "The entire network should function, in terms of its own evaluation and self-improvement, as a 'community of practice' that comes together from time to time (twice a year would be great) to learn from one another's experience."

The process must also be apolitical. "Regional technical assistance centres must remain at arm's length from partisan politics," Bopp warns, "focussing on community healing and development and advocating for what is needed to support the development of the people they work with." In this way, Bopp says, ordinary citizens in Aboriginal communities can get involved, even if their leadership is opposed to the process. "If Aboriginal governments don't want to promote human and community development, then Aboriginal civil society must be supported to do so," he concludes.

Before the Aboriginal Healing Foundation has been completely dismantled, it should be funded to host a series of summits for national Aboriginal organizations, individuals and communities with experience in human and economic development. The groups participating in the summits could devise the best way to implement this recommendation.

2. Create a broad-based citizens' coalition to support the aspirations of Aboriginal Canadians.

Thousands of non-Aboriginal people across the country are appalled at the persistence of unlivable social conditions on reserves and Inuit and Metis communities across the country and the racial tensions created by longstanding land disputes such as the one presently tearing apart the people of Caledonia and Six Nations. I heard from some concerned citizens after my series was published in the *Toronto Star.* Dr. Wigdan Al-Sukhni, a general surgery resident in Toronto, was particularly eloquent in expressing his feelings: "I would like to learn how I can help. I want to be part of the solution. I have always been passionate about human rights, and have been involved with several organizations over the years to raise awareness about human rights violations across the world, especially the atrocities that have occurred in my birth country, Iraq. But the Aboriginal community's suffering takes place in my own backyard, and I think it would be utter hypocrisy on my part to ignore it. I would greatly appreciate any guidance you can offer me as to how I can become involved."

An Innu-Inuit support group was formed in St. John's in the early 1980s. The group held news conferences to publicize the concerns of Labrador's Aboriginal people on a variety of issues and took out newspaper ads to denounce politicians who acted insensitively. This coalition of citizens, academics, church and anti-poverty organizations strengthened the voice of Aboriginal people by giving credibility to their concerns.

As individuals, we can start by meeting the Aboriginal people in our own neighbourhoods, towns and cities, learning from them what needs to be done. Maggie Hodgson envisioned this when she created the National Day of Healing and Reconciliation, held every year on May 26. Collectively, we can pressure the provincial and federal governments to right the historical injustices and ensure that Aboriginal people have an equal place in our society. Governments will do nothing more than they are doing now without an informed, active lobby effort by non-Aboriginal Canadians.

I envision a national group that would meet annually to draw up a list of achievable policies developed in consultation with Aboriginal organizations. The group would then persistently lobby governments to act on these objectives. Possible models are PEN Canada, which advocates on behalf of writers who are persecuted and imprisoned around the world, and Indigenous Survival International, based in London, England, which studies and publicizes issues related to the well-being of Indigenous people. The formation of such a group could be tied to Canada's Truth and Reconciliation process.

3. Fund national Aboriginal organizations to launch a process of consultation in communities across the country, with the assistance of addiction experts, that will lead to a firm policy regarding alcohol consumption, favouring either total abstinence or harm reduction.

Many Aboriginal leaders believe that their people must abstain from alcohol completely. Others favour harm reduction. The Assembly of First Nations, the Inuit Tapiriit Kanatami and the Metis Federation could use existing community NNADAP structures—and the program must be expanded to meet this need—to launch a debate about the relative merits of the two approaches. After community members have been consulted, a firm policy should be adopted by the national organizations. (The Assembly of First Nations and the National Native Addictions Partnership Foundation already support total abstinence.) The policy would then be strictly and consistently applied, and community leaders would make enforcing it a priority.

While this consultation process is under way, a moratorium could be imposed on the shipment of alcohol by air or sea to all remote Aboriginal communities for one year. While this would not stop the flow of alcohol completely, it would reduce supply, particularly if Aboriginal organizations, the provinces and the territorial governments cooperated to put such a moratorium in place. According to Noel Pearson of the Cape York Institute for Policy and Leadership in

Cairns, Australia, alcohol management plans there are having a positive impact. The effectiveness of the moratorium could be reviewed at the end of one year to determine if it should be extended.

The sale of alcohol must also be taken out of the hands of provincial finance departments and made a health department responsibility, as Michael Miltenberger, former minister of Health and Social Services for the Northwest Territories, recommends.

4. Develop a national strategy for the prevention and treatment of Fetal Alcohol Spectrum Disorder.

Dr. Sterling Clarren, director of the Canada-Northwest FASD task force, wants more partners for the work his group is doing. He'd like more cooperation and support from the federal government, and the provinces east of Manitoba, which are not yet part of the alliance. A standard public health policy on the treatment and prevention of FASD is crucial, Clarren says, and now is the time for maximum collaboration and cooperation.

It is not only the Aboriginal community who must be informed about FASD; Clarren says any society that drinks puts its children at risk. With our increased affluence as a society, we also spend more of our disposable income on alcohol. Public education on the dangers of alcohol consumption during pregnancy must be stepped up, and more support must be provided to the people now affected by the problem.

5. Provide national Aboriginal organizations with the funding to create a public education program warning Aboriginal youth of the dangers of binge drinking.

No truly comprehensive public education program of this sort exists at the moment. Health Canada has produced some materials, but the information is rarely made available in Aboriginal languages or in ways that truly engage youth. Many NNADAP community workers told me they lack the training and resources to perform the community education component of their work. Aboriginal writers and artists could be hired to create a slick, youth-oriented campaign that makes it more cool to stay sober than to drink. Public education can be very effective as long as it embodies Aboriginal values and accompanies a community development and healing process.

6. Honour the commitment made in the Kelowna Accord to end the housing shortage in Aboriginal communities within ten years.

The Aboriginal Roundtable to Support the Kelowna Accord estimated in 2005 that there is a need for 35,000 to 40,000 new homes on First Nations reserves. Another 5,000 are needed in Metis and Inuit communities. This finding was reinforced in November 2007 in an alarming report released by the YWCA in Yellowknife on the dire situation of Inuit women who are forced into dangerous relationships simply to put a roof over their heads. The report, "You Just Blink and It Can Happen: A Study of Women's Homelessness North of 60," estimates that at least 1,000 women in the Yukon, the Northwest Territories and Nunavut are homeless, and that 1,000 children "trail along behind them." Nunavut has the country's highest birth rate, along with a waiting list of thousands for social housing. (Private homes are extremely expensive to build in the North, because of permafrost and the high cost of imported building materials.) At least 273 houses a year would need to be built to keep up with demand in Nunavut alone, yet only seventy are budgeted for 2008.

The current housing shortage in Aboriginal communities means many children are living with binge-drinking relatives, putting their safety at risk. Bachelor apartments for problem drinkers and drug users should be provided to offer respite for other family members; these units should come with supervision, security and ready access to detoxification and addiction services.

As a long-term investment, trades training must also be provided to help First Nations and Inuit develop the skills required to build housing in their own communities.

7. Expand services to treat and prevent childhood sexual abuse in Aboriginal communities.

Childhood sexual abuse, much of it learned behaviour from the residential schools, lies at the root of a great deal of the alcoholism, drug use and suicide in Aboriginal communities. There's great willingness on the part of Aboriginal people to stop the cycle; what's missing are the resources to do so. Hollow Water's Community Holistic Circle Healing process and restorative justice models such as the one offered at the Friendship Centre in Hinton, Alberta, have proven their effectiveness. These programs must receive solid funding and be made more widely available. Culturally appropriate treatment models and programs must be developed in First Nation, Inuit and Metis communities, and workers in those communities trained to deliver them. In the Labrador Innu Comprehensive Healing Strategy, for example, few services were provided to help victims of sexual abuse, despite the connection many Innu have made between this issue and the other social problems they are trying to solve. This is an urgent issue, and solutions must be put in place immediately to address it.

8. Provide more opportunities for Aboriginal youth to be mentored and provide more intercultural education for non-Aboriginal teachers and service providers.

Mary Sillett, mayor of the Inuit community of Hopedale, was the first Inuk in Canada to obtain a university degree (she studied social work). For seventeen years she worked in Ottawa as a federal government policy advisor and in leadership roles with national Aboriginal organizations and the Royal Commission on Aboriginal Peoples. Sillett has since returned to Hopedale, her home community, to assist her people. She believes mentorship and quality education are crucial if the children of Aboriginal addicts are to avoid the pitfalls of their parents.

"I came from one of those families where everyone was drinking," she told me. "What saved me were the people outside my home who were extremely strong and influential in the community, and they were always there for me. People such as Reverend Bill Peacock. He was always there for me. The teachers I had in school, I really liked them; they were good to me, and they really encouraged me. And then throughout the years there were groups such as the Knights of Columbus who would give us food when my grandfather couldn't feed us. So that makes a difference in the community."

Reverend Peacock was a Moravian church minister who had a long association with Labrador's Inuit and was respected within their communities. His mentorship of Sillett and others worked because of this background and because of the respect he had for Inuit culture and language. Non-Aboriginal teachers sent into Aboriginal communities need preparation and cultural education if they are to be effective mentors for the children they will be teaching.

Even one significant person in an Aboriginal child's life can make all the difference, according to Wayne Hammond, a Calgary-based psychologist who has worked with many young Aboriginal solvent abusers. Instead of taking young people away from their families, which creates greater social problems, Hammond thinks a formalized mentorship program should be created to help children whose parents are not able to look after them. "Some parents, through no fault of their own, simply will never be able to care for their children, because they can't care for themselves," he told me when I met him in Natuashish.

Hammond suggests that these parents be asked to designate another family member or a trusted friend to stand in for them, so that they can continue to have some involvement in their children's lives. A similar program is shaping up in Australia. Noel Pearson's organization is planning to set up a families' commission in communities on the Cape York Peninsula; the commission will be asked to recommend new caregivers, preferably family members, for children whose parents are using family support payments to buy booze or drugs.

Hammond learned a lot when he worked as a counsellor at Woods Home, a youth solvent-abuse treatment centre in Calgary. "A lot of the children I met didn't know they had strengths, and they didn't know how to celebrate them. They haven't had people or mentors to come alongside and say, 'I like you, and no matter what you do, I'm going to be here and if you want to talk, I'll listen.' If kids have one person in their life who's absolutely crazy about them, who is willing to go the distance with them, they do okay."

Mary Sillett is now a mentor herself to children in her community. "We, the people who are doing well, have to understand that if a child is not doing well at home, at least you can be kind to them. Give them a ride sometimes. Invite them to your home for a meal. Teachers can encourage the students. They don't realize what an impact they can have later on, if those kids do well. It was because of all the kindnesses they met on the way."

9. Create a coordinated national strategy to reduce the sky-rocketing rate of Aboriginal youth suicide.

This was a key recommendation of both the Royal Commission on Aboriginal Peoples and "Out of the Shadows at Last," the report of the 2006 Senate Committee on Mental Health, Mental Illness and Addiction. The Royal Commission's report called for a national strategy that included measures to track the number of deaths by suicide, to conduct research into the causes and to fast-track solutions. When the commission published its research in 1996, it estimated the rate of Aboriginal suicide to be five to six times the Canadian average, and there has been little change in that number, despite the establishment of a Suicide Prevention Advisory Group set up by the First Nations and Inuit Branch of Health Canada in 2001–2002.

As "Out of the Shadows at Last" stated: "The committee does not understand how federal departments, knowing the abysmal health status of Aboriginal peoples and the fact that this population is universally considered to be at risk, could have failed to collect or support others in collecting the data required to develop a strategy to address the problem in a meaningful way and to measure progress subsequently with respect to outcomes." I support the Senate committee's recommendation that "a designated suicide fund that accommodates the distinct needs of each group of Aboriginal people" be allocated immediately.

10. Increase media coverage of Aboriginal issues.

In the summer of 2007 I attended a meeting of CBC journalists in Saskatchewan called "Aboriginal Matters." Those in attendance made a commitment to increase the quantity and quality of CBC's coverage of Aboriginal issues. At the time of writing, CBC News was still without an Ottawa-based reporter specializing in Aboriginal issues, a deficiency I hope will soon be addressed. Currently no Aboriginal columnist writes on a daily or weekly basis for a national newspaper, and Aboriginal journalists across the country are scarce. We need more of them, and this won't happen until mainstream media outlets make recruitment a priority.

Reporting on Aboriginal issues by journalists of all stripes should be stepped up, so that pressure is kept on governments to follow through on their policies and promises. A well-informed public will be a more proactive public. Too often, media coverage of Aboriginal issues happens only when tempers have boiled over. More investigative reporting could help prevent disputes from reaching the crisis point by bringing issues to public attention. Currently, more space and energy in the media are devoted to reporting on the lives of people and cultures outside Canada than on the needs of the diverse Indigenous cultures in our midst.

11. Make the mental health and addiction needs of Aboriginal people an immediate national priority by improving the delivery of health care.

Some of the most heartrending testimony given at the Senate Committee on Mental Health, Mental Illness and Addiction hearings in 2005–2006 came from Aboriginal people. The committee's report, "Out of the Shadows at Last," identified the need for "an unprecedented level of both federal leadership and intergovernmental collaboration to address the epidemic of mental health problems, including suicide and addictions, in Aboriginal communities." The report echoes the call by doctors Cornelia Wieman and

Peter Menzies for better funding for programs directed at Aboriginal mental health and addiction treatment. Adequate care must also be made available in home communities, with fair compensation for health workers on reserve. "We kept many patients out of hospital by providing good community-based care," Wieman told me about her work on the Six Nations reserve near Brantford, Ontario. "But across the country health workers in Aboriginal communities are paid far less than their counterparts off reserve."

In addition, Wieman says, "Many positions for mental health workers in Aboriginal communities are not filled because qualified staff is not available." The national training program that she suggests to address this must be put in place. The addiction treatment centre for Aboriginal leaders that Menzies recommends should also be established, as should a centre of excellence for treating intergenerational trauma; what is learned at such a centre could later be expanded to help the refugees fleeing war-torn countries who are settling in Canada in greater numbers. The recommendations in Pauktuutit's guide "Sharing Knowledge, Sharing Wisdom" should be adopted in the North.

Substantially increasing the number of Aboriginal health professionals was a major recommendation of the Royal Commission on Aboriginal Peoples, and Canada's medical and nursing schools must establish recruitment programs in order to achieve this. Health Canada must also devolve jobs and responsibilities to Aboriginal people. In the case of the Labrador Innu Comprehensive Healing Strategy, this will mean transferring responsibility for the program to the Innu nation.

Finally, NNADAP should be given the additional resources needed to expand its work, particularly in Inuit communities, which for many years were ineligible for NNADAP programs.

12. Establish a national exchange program between Aboriginal and non-Aboriginal youth.

In 1974 and 1975, when I was in my late teens, I travelled from my home in Newfoundland to Quebec on six-week exchange trips paid for by the federal government to promote bilingualism. While I was at university in Newfoundland, I made friends with students from Quebec who'd taken advantage of the same opportunity. A similar national exchange program to promote biculturalism and enhance understanding among Aboriginal and non-Aboriginal youth could be similarly successful. It would be enriching for the teens and would help create a new generation of non-Aboriginal Canadians with a better understanding of the unique and beautiful cultures that evolved in this country thousands of years ago.

INTRODUCTION

John Gray's op-ed piece on Davis Inlet, "Natuashish: Back to Square One," was published in the *Globe and Mail* on March 8, 2005. It is held in an online archive at www.diversitywatch.ryerson.ca/media/cache/natuashish_globe_mar8.htm. Statistics Canada's 2006 census results on the Aboriginal population, published in January 2008, can be found at www.statcan.ca/Daily/English/080115/ d080115a.htm. While much media attention was paid to the fact the results showed the Aboriginal population at 1,172,790 people, the Indian and Northern Affairs Canada Web site has indicated the Aboriginal population at more than 1 million for several years. When I wrote my series for the *Toronto Star*, I used the population numbers provided by INAC at that time—1,391,000.

CHAPTER 1: HEALING THE SPIRIT

An evaluation of the Fifth Healing Our Spirit Worldwide conference, held August 6 to 11, 2006, in Edmonton, Alberta, was published in the fall 2006 issue of the web-based journal, *Pimatisiwin,* available online at www.pimatisi win.com/Articles/4.2H_Healing_Our_Spirit.pdf. It was prepared and written by Cheryl Currie, Nancy Gibson and Patti LaBoucane-Benson for the Addiction and Mental Health Research Laboratory at the University of Alberta in Edmonton. The plenary sessions and many of the workshops were recorded on audio and are available for sale online at www.kennedyrecordings.com/conf/heal ing2006.htm or by calling toll free 1-888-486-1335. There are three Canadian members of the International Indigenous Council that organizes Healing Our Spirit Worldwide events. They are Rod Jeffries (avisions@sympatico.ca), Chief Austin Bear (info@nnapf.org) and Allen Benson (allen-benson@ncsa. ca). Maggie Hodgson has her own Web site with links to her articles, including "From Anomie to Recovery" and "Rebuilding Community after the Residential School Experience." Her Web site is www.maggiehodgson.com. The Indian Residential Schools Resolutions Canada Web site is www.irsr-rqpi.gc.ca and it contains a lot of information about the residential school settlement package. The National Day of Healing and Reconciliation Web site is www.ndhr.ca.

CHAPTER 2: A FRIGHTENING PROGNOSIS

My series, "Tragedy or Triumph: Canadian Public Policy and Aboriginal Addictions," appeared in the *Toronto Star* in November and December 2006 and at the time of this writing is still available online at http://thestar.com/atkinson. I interviewed Dr. Ted Rosales in St. John's in the fall of 2006. The First Nations and Inuit Health Committee of the Canadian Paediatric Society describe the effects of FASD that I cite in this chapter. The Web site source is www.cps.ca/english/statements/II/ii02-01.htm#Clinical%20manifestations. The Web site for the Canada Northwest FASD Partnership is www.cnfasdpartnership.ca. Michael Dorris's *The Broken Cord: A Family's Ongoing Struggle with Fetal Alcohol Syndrome* was published in Toronto by HarperCollins Canada in 1989. My trip to Natuashish and my conversation with Victoria Rich took place in December 2005. Wayne Hammond was in the community at that time. He has co-founded a non-profit organization based in Calgary called Resiliency Canada, whose Web site is www.resiliencycanada.ca. A copy of the IER Planning, Research and Management Services and the Aboriginal Research Institute's interim evaluation of the Labrador Innu Comprehensive Healing Strategy, 2003, is available online at www.ainc-inac.gc.ca/pr/pub/ae/ev/01-28/01-28_03_e.html. The Nechi Training, Research and Health Promotion Institute maintains a Web site at www.nechi.com. The National Aboriginal Health Organization (NAHO) has published a National Report of the First Nations and Inuit Regional Health Survey, 1999, available online at www.icah.ca/content/en/resources/detail/index. php?rid=62385. It concludes that, until a comparison of the prevalent rates of FAS for Natives and non-Natives has been carried out, it will be impossible to say if rates are higher in Aboriginal communities. I interviewed Michael Miltenberger, who was then the minister of health for the Northwest Territories, in the spring of 2006. I interviewed Dr. Sterling Clarren in the fall of 2006.

CHAPTER 3: A BIRTHDAY PARTY

My primary source for the statement that more Aboriginals abstain completely from alcohol than in the general population comes from the First Nations Regional Longitudinal Health Survey 2002–2003 *Report on Selected Indicators by Gender*, available online at www.rhs-ers.ca/english/phase1.asp. It found that 17.8 per cent of First Nations adults consume alcohol on a daily or weekly basis, compared to 44 per cent in the general population. It also reported that 34 per cent of First Nations adults abstain completely from alcohol compared with 21 per cent who abstain in the general population. This information is contained as well in Richard Thatcher's book, *Fighting Firewater Fictions: Moving beyond the Disease Model of Addiction in First Nations*, published in Toronto by the University of Toronto Press in 2004. Thatcher edits the magazine *Circle Talk*, which contains up-to-date information of help to community workers in the area of Aboriginal mental health and addiction treatment and prevention programs. Funding is provided by Health Canada. A subscription can be obtained by emailing Cherylee Highway of the Saskatchewan Indian Institute of Technology at highwayc@siit.sk.ca. Anestasia Shkilnyk's book, *A Poison Stronger than Love: The Destruction of an Ojibwa Community*, was published in New Haven, Connecticut, by Yale University Press in 1985. Brian Maracle's book, *Crazywater: Native Voices on Addiction and Recovery*, was published in Toronto by Penguin Canada in 1994. I interviewed Barney Williams Jr. at the NNADAP banquet, held during the Assembly of First Nations annual general meeting in Vancouver in June 2006. Sharon Clarke spoke to me at the 2006 Healing Our Spirit Worldwide conference. Carol Hopkins is running the National Native Addictions Partnership Foundation while Clarke is away on study leave. The NNAPF Web site is www.nnapf.org and a history of the NNADAP program is posted on the Health Canada Web site at www.hc-sc.gc.ca/fnih-spni/substan/ads/nnadap-pnlaada_e.html.

The 1998 review of the NNADAP program that makes many fine recommendations that have yet to be completely implemented is available also through Health Canada at www.hc-sc.gc.ca/fnih-spni/pubs/ads/1998_rpt-nnadap-pnlaada/5_summary-sommaire_e.html.

CHAPTER 4: A CRIPPLING AFFLICTION

The 2002–2003 First Nations Regional Longitudinal Health Survey was prepared by the First Nations Health Centre of the National Aboriginal Health Organization and released in 2005. It provides a clear and honest picture of the addiction and other health problems in Canada's First Nation

communities and is available at www.naho.ca/firstnations/english/documents/
RHS200203TechnicalReport_000.pdf. More information about this survey
can be found at http://rhs-ers.ca/english/background-governance.asp. A
separate study for First Nations in Quebec, "Quebec Regions First Nations
Regional Longitudinal Health Survey," conducted in 2002 and published
in 2006, is available on the First Nations of Quebec and Labrador Health
and Social Services Commission website at www.cssspnql.com/cssspnql/ui/
strategy/StrategyHealthSurvey.jsp?section=link_strategy&lang=_en. One of
the best sources for Inuit is the 2004 study, "Alcohol Problems and Approaches:
Theories, Evidence and Northern Practice," prepared by Marja Korhonen for the
Ajuunginiq Centre of the National Aboriginal Health Organization and available
online at www.naho.ca/english/pdf/alcohol_problems_approaches.pdf. For
more information on the Innu culture, a fine Web site was created to accompany
Pien Penashue's canoe exhibit at The Rooms, the Newfoundland and Labrador
museum in St. John's; it can be viewed at www.tipatshimuna.ca. My book,
Nitassinan: The Innu Struggle to Reclaim Their Homeland, published in Vancouver
by Douglas and McIntyre in 1991 and reissued in 2001, documents Innu
opposition to the militarization of northern Quebec and Labrador. The Centre for
Addiction and Mental Health in Toronto has prepared *Aboriginal Peoples: Mental
Health and Substance Misuse Selected Bibliography,* found on the web at www.camh.
net/About_Addiction_Mental_Health/CAMH_Library/AboriginalBib2004.pdf.
Addiction isn't just an Aboriginal problem; it's just more serious because of the
peoples' recent history of dependency. "Answering the Call," a report calling for
a national action plan to reduce alcohol and drug addiction was prepared by the
Drug Strategy and Controlled Substances Programme of the Canadian Centre on
Substance Abuse and published in 2005; it is available online at www.ccsa.ca/
NR/rdonlyres/4F0512B8-C7A3-4019-B6C2-55497F837A9F/0/ccsa0113222005.
pdf. *The Insanity of Alcohol: Social Problems in Canadian First Nations Communities*
was written by Paul Whitehead and Michael Hayes and published in Toronto
by Canadian Scholars' Press in 1998. I also enjoyed reading Nancy Oestreich
Lurie's famous essay, "The World's Oldest On-Going Protest Demonstration:
North American Indian Drinking Patterns," *Pacific Historical Review,* vol. 40,
no. 3 (August 1971), pp. 311–332. I had personal communication with Enid
Harrison at the Canadian Centre on Substance Abuse in which she expressed
regret that the addiction survey it conducts only takes place every ten years
and that it doesn't break down numbers for the Aboriginal population. Another
source I used here was Statistics Canada's 1991 Aboriginal Peoples Survey,
available online at www.statcan.ca/english/Dli/Data/Ftp/aps.htm.

CHAPTER 5: A FAMILY'S TRIUMPH OVER ADDICTION

The Brentwood Recovery Home's Web site is www.brentwoodrecovery.com. Dr. Laurence Kirmayer is the Director of McGill University's Division of Social and Transcultural Psychiatry and editor-in-chief of the journal, *Transcultural Psychiatry*, available online at tps.sagepub.com. Elizabeth Penashue (Tshaukuesh) received an Aboriginal Achievement Award for environmental activism in March 2008.

CHAPTER 6: WHAT ADDICTS HAVE IN COMMON

Dr. Wilfred Gallant's book about Father Charbonneau and the Brentwood Recovery Home, *Sharing the Love that Frees Us: A Spiritual Awakening from the Struggles of Addiction and Abuse*, was published in Concord, Ontario, by Captus Press in 1992. I did my interviews at Brentwood in January 2006. I found George Vaillant's *The Natural History of Alcoholism* helpful for this chapter as well. It was published in Cambridge, Massachusetts, by Harvard University Press in 1995.

CHAPTER 7: THE MIRACLE AT ALKALI LAKE

DVD copies of *The Honour of All* are available from Filmwest Associates online at *www.filmwest.com* or toll free at 1-888-982-3456. It was produced in 1985 by Phil Lucas and Phil Lane Jr. of Four Worlds International. Lane has many useful resources to help Aboriginals in recovery on his Web site at www.four worlds.ca. Highlights of the 2006 United Nations Human Development Index are available at www.infoplease.com/ipa/A0778562.html and the entire study is located at http://hdr.undp.org/en/statistics/. The Assembly of First Nations "Make Poverty History" campaign is now underway, with more information on the financial situation of First Nations communities available at http://www. afn.ca/article.asp?id=2903. Phil Fontaine's "The Native Fiscal Imbalance," was published in the *Globe and Mail* on October 30, 2006, and is available online at http://media.knet.ca/node/2308. My figures on the poverty rates in British Columbia and how they compare with other provinces come from the National Council of Welfare, "Welfare Incomes, 2000 and 2001," available online at www.ncwcnbes.net/documents/researchpublications/ResearchProjects/ WelfareIncomes/2000-01Report_Spring2002/ENG/ReportENG.htm. My information on the history of the St. Joseph's Residential school near Williams Lake, B.C., comes from the Law Commission of Canada's report,

"Restoring Dignity: Responding to Child Abuse in Canadian Institutions," available online at http://epe.lac-bac.gc.ca/100/206/301/law_commission_of_canada-ef/2006-12-06/www.lcc.gc.ca/research_project/ica/report/restoring-1-en.asp. I also read the Public Health Agency of Canada report, "Toward a Healthy Future," available online at www.phac-aspc.gc.ca/ph-sp/phdd/report/toward/back/how.html. Naomi Adelson, a medical anthropologist at York University, has written passionately about how Aboriginal poverty puts the people at risk in her book, *Being Alive Well: Health and Politics of Cree Well-Being*, published in Toronto by the University of Toronto Press in 2000, and in "The Embodiment of Inequity: Health Disparities in Aboriginal Canada," *Canadian Journal of Public Health*, vol. 96, suppl. 2 (March–April 2005), pp. S45–S61, available online at http://pubs.cpha.ca/PDF/P24/22247.pdf. Find out more about Dr. Laurence Kirmayer's theory of Aboriginals "ecocentrism" in "Psychotherapy and the Cultural Concept of the Person," *Transcultural Psychiatry*, vol. 44, no. 2 (June 2007), pp. 232–257.

CHAPTER 8: HEALING IN HOLLOW WATER

The Corrections Canada report on the history and effectiveness of Community Holistic Circle Healing, "The Four Circles of Hollow Water," is available at http://ww2.ps-sp.gc.ca/publications/abor_corrections/199703_e.pdf. Christine Sivell-Ferri was a contract researcher at the time and is now teaching in Ontario's Georgian Bay district. Dr. William Marshall and Y.M. Fernandez's comments are from the same Corrections Canada study. Dereck O'Brien's book, *Suffer Little Children: Unlocking the Memories of Pain and Abuse*, was published in St. John's by Breakwater Books in 1991. I interviewed Burma Bushie one evening during the Healing Our Spirit Worldwide conference. My other interviews on the CHCH process were conducted while I was in the community in the winter of 2006. Ed Buller's essay, "A Cost-Benefit Analysis of Hollow Water First Nation's Community Holistic Healing Process," in *Aboriginal Policy Research: Setting the Agenda for Change*, vol. 2, edited by Jerry White, Paul Maxim and Dan Beavon, was published in Toronto by Thompson Educational in 2004. The Indian and Northern Affairs Web site posts a useful document, "Measuring the Well-Being of Aboriginal People: An Application of the United Nations' Human Development Index to Registered Indians in Canada, 1981–2001," edited by Martin Cooke, Daniel Beavon and Mindy McHardy, available at www.ainc-inac.gc.ca/pr/ra/mwb/index_e.html. I interviewed Marcel Hardisty at Wanipigow, Hollow Water, Manitoba, in May 2006.

CHAPTER 9: THE TRAUMA CONNECTION

I read Maria Yellow Horse Brave Heart's article, "The Historical Trauma Response among Natives and Its Relationship to Substance Abuse," in *Healing and Mental Health for Native Americans: Speaking in Red,* edited by Ethan Nebelkopf and Mary Phillips and published in Lanham, Maryland, by Rowman and Littlefield in 2004, also available at *www.columbia.edu/cu/ssw/faculty/ profiles/braveheart.html.* I interviewed Dr. Cornelia Wieman and Dr. Peter Menzies in January 2006. The work of Dr. Clare Brant is described in an article by Cornelia Wieman published on the Web site of the Canadian Psychiatric Association at http://ww1.cpa-apc.org:8080/Publications/Archives/CJP/2000/ Sep/Brant.asp. Peter Mancall's book, *Deadly Medicine: Indians and Alcohol in Early America,* was published in Ithaca, New York, by Cornell University Press in 1995. Mancall, a professor of history at the University of Southern California and one of his specialties is early Native American Indian history (c. 1492 to 1840), offers a comprehensive history of the relationship Aboriginals in North America have with alcohol. I interviewed Dr. Sousan Abadian and Dr. Jane Simington at the Healing Our Spirit Worldwide conference in Edmonton in 2006. The Royal Commission on Aboriginal Peoples, 1996, has made many fine recommendations about the need for more Aboriginal health professionals in Canada. The Commission's reports are available online at www.ainc-inac.gc.ca/ ch/rcap/sg/sgmm_e.html or in hard copy at most libraries.

CHAPTER 10: MOVING FROM PAIN TO HOPE

The late Norwegian anthropologist, Georg Henricksen, who lived in Davis Inlet in 1967 when the Mushuau Innu were first settled there, wrote the seminal book on these people, *Hunters in the Barrens: The Naskapi on the Edge of the White Man's World,* published in St. John's, Newfoundland, by the Institute for Social and Economic Research at Memorial University in 1973. As well, Colin Samson has written about the Innu and their substance abuse problems in *A Way of Life That Does Not Exist: Canada and the Extinguishment of the Innu,* published in London by Verso Press in 2003. My information that the crewmembers of the HMV *Bonavista* sold alcohol to the people of Davis Inlet came from personal communication after I was invited to speak to some retired crewmembers in 1992. An important essay by Peter Penashue, "Healing the Past, Meeting the Future," is included in *Aboriginal Autonomy and Development in Northern Quebec and Labrador,* edited by Colin Scott and published in Vancouver by the University of British Columbia Press in 2001. Indian and Northern Affairs have posted an independent evaluation of the Labrador Innu Comprehensive Healing Strategy on its Web site at www.ainc-inac.gc.ca/pr/pub/ae/ev/01-28/01-28_e.html. I interviewed George Gregoire Sr. and Sgt. Grant Smith while I was in Natuashish in December 2005.

CHAPTER 11: SEEKING SOLUTIONS DOWN UNDER

"The Dark Side of Australia's Palm Island" by Andrew Boe, published in the online journal, *Countercurrents,* on March 17, 2005, and available at www.countercur rents.org/hr-boe170305.htm, is the source of my information at the opening of this chapter. I also read an article by Cara Page and John Mceachran, "I Love Life on Danger Island," in Scotland's *The Daily Record* in 2006, about a Scottish nun who lives on Palm Island and has dedicated her life to helping the people. I recently found a reprint of the article on a blog at http://britishexpats.com/forum/showthread.php?t=398924&page=2. Noel Pearson's ideas and speeches are contained on the Cape York Institute's Web site at www.cyi.org.au and at www.capeyorkpartnerships.com/team/noelpearson/papers.htm. His book, *Our Right to Take Responsibility,* published in Cairns, Queensland, by Noel Pearson and Associates in 2000, can be ordered online at www.brisinst.org.au/pdf/pearsonbook.pdf. Also instructional is the transcript of an interview Pearson gave Paul Barclay of the Australian Broadcasting Corporation in October 2000, available online at www.abc.net.au/rn/backgroundbriefing/stories/2000/203074.htm. John Pilger's *The New Rulers of the World,* published in London by Verso in 2002, is also excellent reading on the status of Australia's Aboriginal population. The article "Land Where Petrol Fuels Nothing but Despair" by Ashleigh Wilson (August 13, 2005) is available online in the archives of the newspaper *The Australian* at www.theaustralian.news.com.au/story/0,25197,16243092-2702,00. html. A Canadian book by Calvin Helin, *Dances with Dependency: Indigenous Success through Self-reliance,* published in Vancouver by Orca Spirit Publishing in 2006, contains many ideas similar to Noel Pearson's. Helin is a member of the Tsimshian nation. His website is www.spiritorca.com.

CHAPTER 12: HEARTACHE IN KENORA

I interviewed Ozzie Suenath, Tania Cameron and Charles McDonald when I was in Kenora, Ontario, in May 2006. The Kenora Chiefs Advisory maintains a Web site at www.kenorachiefs.ca. Tania Cameron is a band councillor at the Dalles First Nation (Ochiichagwe'babigo'ining), one of Canada's most populous reserves with a population over 6,000. She's also the NDP candidate for Kenora in the next federal election. Reg Clayton wrote about the World Sui-cide Prevention day vigil organized by Tania Cameron in "Suicide prevention focus of local World Health Organization event," *Kenora Daily Miner and News,* September 12, 2005, available online at http://cgi.bowesonline.com/pedro.php?id=3&x=story&xid=183709.

The Senate Committee on Mental Health, Mental Illness and Addiction released the report, "Out of the Shadows at Last: Transforming Mental Health, Mental Illness and Addiction Services in Canada" in May 2006, and it is available online at www.parl.gc.ca/39/1/parlbus/commbus/senate/com-e/soci-e/rep-e/rep02may06-e.htm. I used the First Nations Inuit Health Branch of Health Canada study, "Acting on What We Know: Preventing Youth Suicide in First Nations," available at www.hc-sc.gc.ca/fnih-spni/pubs/suicide/prev_youth-jeunes/index_e.html, for some background to this chapter. The report, "The Health of Canada's Children," published in Ottawa by the Canadian Institute of Child Health in 2000, compared First Nations and Canadian suicide rates from 1989 to 1993 for ages birth to fourteen and fifteen to twenty-four. The rate of First Nations youth suicide given there is among First Nations men between the ages of fifteen to twenty-four years. It was 126 per 100,000, compared to 24 per 100,000 for Canadian men of the same age group; young women from First Nations registered a rate of 35 per 100,000 versus only 5 per 100,000 for Canadian women. The anecdote about flooding One Man Lake comes from Brian K. Smith's "Wabaseemoong Case Study: Appropriate Education in a First Nations Reserve School," a master's thesis for St. Francis Xavier University completed in 1995 and submitted to the Royal Commission on Aboriginal Peoples the same year. Smith taught on the Wabaseemoong First Nation reserve at Whitedog, Ontario. The entire thesis is available at www.collectionscanada.ca/obj/s4/f2/dsk2/ftp04/mq23771.pdf .

CHAPTER 13: ADDICTION, VIOLENCE AND THE THREAT TO INUIT WOMEN
I spoke with Lavinia Piercey in Nain in November 2006. Pauktuutit's 2006 report, "National Strategy to Prevent Abuse in Inuit Communities," is published at www.pauktuutit.ca/pdf/publications/abuse/InuitStrategy_e.pdf. I visited the offices of this agency representing Inuit women during the winter of 2006 and spoke with Jennifer Dickson and met some of the staff involved in the anti-violence strategy. I met addiction workers from Inuit communities in Ottawa that same month and attended one of their workshops. There are conflicting statistics on the life expectancy of Aboriginals. Statistics Canada says it's 68.9 years of age

for men and 76.3 for women (compared to 75 and 81 for non-Aboriginal men and women respectively). However the Inuit Tapiriit Kanatami reports that the life expectancy for Inuit men is 62.6 years and for Inuit women, just 71. Statistics Canada's "Measuring Violence against Women, Statistical Trends," was published in 2006 and is available on the agency's Web site at www.statcan.ca/english/research/85-570-XIE/85-570-XIE2006001.pdf. Excellent information has been collected by the National Aboriginal Health Organization's Ajunnginiq Centre and is available online at www.naho.ca/inuit/e/. The Canadian Centre for Justice Statistics, as part of the federal government's family violence initiative, tracks the number of women who use transitional houses or shelters from violence at http://uregina.ca/datalibrary/holdings/justice.html. The violence issue was raised at the National Aboriginal Women's Summit in Corner Brook, Newfoundland, in June 2007; a summary of the issues discussed is available online at www.laa.gov.nl.ca/laa/naws/pdf/AbuseIssues.pdf. CBC North carried a story about violence in Kangirsuk shortly before I arrived there in March 2006; read it online at www.cbc.ca/canada/north/story/2006/02/06/kangir-violence-06022006.html. The *Nunatsiaq News* is also an excellent source for information on what's happening in Canada's Inuit communities today; they maintain a good archive of stories at www.nunatsiaq.coms. The Statistics Canada report on Family Violence in Canada can be located at the Statistics Canada website at www.statcan.ca/english/freepub/85-224-XIE/85-224-XIE2007000.pdf. The "Sharing Knowledge, Sharing Wisdom" report outlining abuse prevention strategies is posted on the Pauktuutit Web site at www.Pauktuutit.ca. Mary Simon's article "Sovereignty in the North" was published in the November 2007 issue of in *The Walrus* magazine and is available online at www.walrusmagazine.com/articles/2007.11-arctic-canada/. I spoke with Jack Anawak in Kangirsuk, Nunavik, while on the Arctic tour sponsored by the Inuit Tapiriit Kanatami; visit their Web site at www.itk.ca. Anawak's job as Canada's Ambassador to the Circumpolar Affairs has since been abolished despite objections from Canada's Inuit.

CHAPTER 14: FINDING STRENGTH IN INUIT CULTURE

The Ivakkak dog team event is described in detail at www.ivakkak.com/eng/. The financial backers of Ivakkak, the Makivik Corporation, host a Web site at www.makivik.org. An inquiry into the deaths of Inuit sled dogs in Nunavut is now under way, led by a former judge in Newfoundland and Labrador, James Igloliorte. I interviewed RCMP director Doug Reti in May 2006. I read about the L'Université de Québec a Trois Rivières study on addiction levels in Nunavik in an article by Greg Younger-Lewis, "Nunavik addiction goes under the microscope," published in the *Nunatsiaq News,* on March 26, 2004, and available online at www.nunatsiaq.com/archives/40326/news/nunavik/40326_03.html. Younger-Lewis published the preliminary results that I quote. As of January 2008, the final report had not been published.

CHAPTER 15: THE POWER OF POLITICAL WILL IN THE NORTHWEST TERRITORIES
Dr. Jennifer Chalmers' 2002 report, "A State of Emergency: A Report on the Delivery of Addiction Services in the NWT," is available on the Northwest Territories Health and Social Services Web site at www.hlthss.gov.nt.ca/content/Publications/pubresult.asp?ID=196. Her 2006 followup report, "Stay the Course...and Together We Can Secure the Foundation That Has Been Built," is available at www.hlthss.gov.nt.ca/pdf/reports/mental_health_and_addictions/2005/english/stay_the_course/chalmers_summary_report_december_2005.pdf. An updated version of the Northwest Territories report on Alcohol and Drug Abuse is available on the Northwest Territories Health and Social Services Web site at www.hlthss.gov.nt.ca/pdf/reports/mental_health_and_addictions/2006/english/nwt_addiction_survey.pdf. Find the 2006 Northwest Territories Addiction Survey at www.hlthss.gov.nt.ca/pdf/reports/mental_health_and_addictions/2006/english/nwt_addiction_survey.pdf. The Canadian Centre on Substance Abuse has posted details of its partnership with the NWT at www.ccsa.ca/NR/rdonlyres/7020B980-40D1-461E-8F77-CA183A08EF4C/0/ccsaactnew16n12006e.pdf. Find out more about the 2005 Liquor Act Review for the Northwest Territories in the report, "Improving Liquor Legislation in the NWT," available online at www.fin.gov.nt.ca/liquor_act_review/files/liquor%20act%20review%20final%20report.pdf. Further, the Canadian Centre on Substance Abuse published a 2006 study, "The Costs of Substance Abuse in Canada, 2002," available online at www.ccsa.ca/NR/rdonlyres/18F3415E-2CAC-4D21-86E2-CEE549EC47A9/0/ccsa0113322006.pdf.

CHAPTER 16: HEALTH CANADA: ADDICTED TO CONTROL
Two evaluations of the Labrador Innu Comprehensive Healing Strategy are available online. The Planning, Research and Management Services and the Aboriginal Research Institute's interim evaluation is posted on the Indian and Northern Affairs Web site, as cited in the source note to Chapter Two, at www.ainc-inac.gc.ca/pr/pub/ae/ev/01-28/01-28_03_e.html. A second report, "Beginning the Journey to Change: Draft Evaluation of the Community Health

Component of the Labrador Innu Comprehensive Healing Strategy," was completed by Memorial University's Health Research Unit in 2003 and is posted online at www.mun.ca. The Labrador projects of the Tshikapisk Foundation give Aboriginal youth something to do besides drink and projects such as this might be supported by concerned service clubs, individuals and governments; find out more at www.tshikapisk.ca. Dr. Pamela Jumper-Thurman, a Native American academic at the University of Colorado, describes her community readiness for change model in Pamela Jumper-Thurman and Barbara Plested, "Community Readiness: A Model for Healing in a Rural Alaskan Community," in *The Family Psychologist*, Summer 2000, pp. 8–9, and at www.ihs.gov/nonmedicalprograms/nspn/File/community_readiness_model_AK.pdf.

CHAPTER 17: AFFIRMATIVE ACTION IN BRITISH COLUMBIA

Monte Solberg made his now famous statement about the Kelowna Accord on CJWW radio in Saskatchewan. His exact quote is: "The [Kelowna] Accord is something they crafted at the last moment on the back of a napkin on the eve of an election. We're not going to honour that." The Library of Parliament has a record of the negotiations from the Aboriginal Round Table to the Kelowna Accord 2004–2006 and they're available online at www.parl.gc.ca/information/library/PRBpubs/prb0604-e.htm, including a fairly extensive list of the financial commitments that were made. Mary Simon's article "Sovereignty from the North," published in *The Walrus* in November 2007 and available online, as cited in the source note to Chapter 13, expresses disappointment that the accord was not honoured and explains the impact on Inuit communities. Tom Flanagan's book, *First Nations? Second Thoughts*, was published in Montreal by McGill-Queen's University Press in 2000. Marci McDonald wrote a wonderful critique of the book for *The Walrus* in October 2004, called "The Man behind Stephen Harper." British Columbia's affirmative Aboriginal policy is articulated by its Ministry of Aboriginal Relations and Reconciliation. Find a link to the "New Relationship with First Nations Aboriginal People" report, as well as to the throne speech, on the ministry's Web site at www.gov.bc.ca/arr/.

CHAPTER 18: COMMUNITY PLANNING: A WAY OUT OF ADDICTION

I interviewed Levi Southwind and Chief Paul Eshkakogan in Sagamok at the end of March and early April 2006. The Alberta-based NGO called Four Worlds Centre for Development and Learning has important research on its

Web site, especially a history of the Aboriginal recovery movement in Canada called "Mapping the Healing Journey," co-authored by Michael Bopp, Judie Bopp and Phil Lane Jr., published in 2002 and available as a free download on the Publications page at *www.fourworlds.ca*. The Bopps' book, *Recreating the World: A Practical Guide to Building Sustainable Communities,* was reissued in 2007 and is available for sale from the Four Worlds Web site. Many other fine research papers are also available from this organization. The Four Worlds International Institute is a separate organization; visit www.4worlds.org. The "What Was Never Told" workshop proved to be life changing for Brenda Rivers and others at Sagamok. It was designed and presented by Robert Antone of the Oneida Nation and Jim Dumont, an Ojibway, in 1997.

CHAPTER 19: IMPLEMENTING A NATIONAL STRATEGY

Auditor General Sheila Fraser's 2006 Status Report on Management of Programs for First Nations is available at www.oag-bvg.gc.ca/domino/reports.nsf/html/20060505ce.html. Patrick Kelly was director for strategic planning and communication for the B.C. region of Indian and Northern Affairs Canada when he outlined his strategy in the paper, "Investing in Change: First Nations Comprehensive Community Planning," presented to the Aboriginal Policy Research Conference in Ottawa on March 23, 2006. Part of Kelly's plan was implemented in British Columbia, as described on the INAC Web site at http://ainc-inac.gc.ca/bc/fnbc/sucsty/crgn/ccp/ccp_e.html. Dan Yarymowich, director of strategic priorities and communication for INAC in Atlantic Canada, also presented a paper, "Life after Planning: Implementing First Nation Comprehensive Community Plans," at the Aboriginal Research Policy Conference on March 23, 2006. In September 2007, the Membertou First Nation in Nova Scotia received an award for excellence in community development at the province's Celebrating Communities Conference. Membertou is considered a success story in Atlantic Canada; find out more at www.membertou.ca. Other First Nation reserves around the country use the same model; for an example in Saskatchewan, see http://ccbp.architectureandplanning.dal.ca/index.html.

CHAPTER 20: THE ABORIGINAL HEALING FOUNDATION

The Aboriginal Healing Foundation Web site at *www.ahf.ca* hosts an extensive library of original research, including Bill Mussell's *Warrior-Caregivers: Understanding the Challenges and Healing of First Nations Men.* Every publication listed on the Web site's Publications pages will be helpful to researchers interested in social healing issues in Canada's Aboriginal communities. Find out more about the Legacy of Hope's "Where Are the Children" exhibit at www.wherearethechildren.ca and www.legacyofhope.ca. The seminal book on the history of residential schools in Canada is based on research done for the Royal Commission on Aboriginal Peoples by John Milloy. Entitled *A National Crime: The Canadian Government and the Residential School System, 1879 to 1986*, it was published in Winnipeg by the University of Manitoba Press in 1999. Information on the Mamowichihitowin program comes from personal communication with Lisa Higgerty following her workshop at the Healing Our Spirit Worldwide conference in August 2006. A link to Canada's Truth and Reconciliation Commission can be found on the Indian Residential Schools Resolution Canada Web site at www.irsr-rqpi.gc.ca/english/truth_reconciliation_commission.html.

CHAPTER 21: LESSONS FROM OLD CROW

Find out more about the Old Crow community on their Web site at *www.oldcrow.ca* and on the Vuntut Gwitchin First Nation Web site at www.vgfn.ca. The people of Old Crow demonstrate the strengths that Chris Lalonde and Mike Chandler write about suicide prevention in Aboriginal communities in their seminal paper, "Cultural Continuity as a Hedge against Suicide in Canada's First Nations Youth," *Transcultural Psychiatry*, vol. 35, no. 2 (June 1998), pp. 191–219, available online at http://web.uvic.ca/~lalonde/manuscripts/1998TransCultural.pdf. Dr. Gail Valaskakis's presentation to the Senate Committee on Mental Health and Addiction is included in the Proceedings of the Standing Senate Committee on Social Affairs, Science and Technology First Session, 38th Parliament, 2004–05 (September 20, 2005), issue no. 27, available online at www.parl.gc.ca/38/1/parlbus/commbus/senate/com-e/soci-e/27cv-e.htm?Language=E&Parl=38&Ses=1&comm_id=47.

Acknowledgements

I WOULD LIKE TO THANK MY EDITOR, BARBARA PULLING, WHOSE enthusiasm supported me through some dark moments and whose top-notch editing skills helped bring to life my vision for this book. Mike Simpson and Lynn McAuley edited the material that first appeared in the *Toronto Star*. I'm indebted to Elizabeth Chan at the Atkinson Charitable Foundation for her kindness and support throughout my tenure as the foundation's 2006 journalism fellow. The Atkinson Fellowship was sponsored by the Atkinson Charitable Foundation, the *Toronto Star* and the Honderich family. Thanks as well to Charles Pascal, Peter Armstrong and John Honderich for giving me this opportunity. Many of my colleagues at the Canadian Broadcasting Corporation supported me, as did my father, Brian, whose mantra "Finish the book" kept me going. My friend Barbara Fitzgerald provided support and encouragement when it was most needed. My children, Nick and Naomi, saw too much of my back as I typed at the computer, but they realized the importance of this project, as did my husband, Chris, who kept things going at home while I travelled. My deepest appreciation goes to the Aboriginal people whose wisdom enriches the pages of this book. I hope my effort here will help to build the public support that is needed for the hard work ahead.

Index